"Thank you, Brother LaPierre, for writing *God's Gift of Imagination*. This book of Christian essays for critical thinking was greatly uplifting to me. I was blessed, convicted, and challenged concerning the need for Biblical truths and convictions, in all areas, in the day in which we live. The candor and your transparency will be of encouragement to the reader."

   —**Paul W. Anderson,** Retired Pastor and Itinerant Preacher
   (Lewiston, Maine)

"Are you a Christian leader who has felt the pressure of the world and culture around you? If so, let *God's Gift of Imagination* by Michael LaPierre refresh your spirit and point you back to foundational principles in the Bible to develop a Christian worldview. His use of Scripture coupled with personal illustrations and applications provide a warmth and honesty that will encourage you to see the world as God sees it."

   —**Dr. Alton Beal**, President, Ambassador Baptist College

"Mike LaPierre writes with great biblical insight, a healthy balance, and a clarity of communication that is needed in our present day. His call to critical thinking is refreshing. You may not come to every conclusion the author does, but he will challenge you to define what you believe biblically and logically."

   —**Pastor Jim Davidson**, Senior Pastor, Maranatha Baptist
   Church (Shelby, North Carolina)

I0079179

"Brace yourself for heard-earned and heart-felt wisdom! One part leadership manual, one part devotional reflection, and one part autobiography, LaPierre's *The Gift of Imagination* invites its readers to reflect on their relationships with God, God's Word, and God's people. Its essays are thought-provoking and earnest, allowing readers to see into his deep wellspring of experiences: from his professional sports career to his career in business to his leadership consulting. All of this is bound together with his deep commitment to his faith and his Savior."

—**Dr. Gene Fant**, President, North Greenville University

"Michael LaPierre's humble spirit shines as he shares his testimony of how the Lord has shaped and uniquely equipped him to make an impact in an increasingly secular society. He shares practical ways every believer can get off the sidelines and actively engage people with the transforming gospel of Jesus Christ. Sustained and guided by God's Word, Christian laymen are urged to be a shining beacon of Christian leadership."

—**John Heffernan**, Senior Pastor, Victory Baptist Church (Simpsonville, South Carolina)

"*God's Gift of Imagination* is an excellent book to challenge and encourage Christians to pursue a deeper, more intimate relationship with Jesus Christ. Many of us become complacent in our journeys as Christians, and Michael LaPierre provides a bold and practical pursuit of the critical-thinking skills necessary to take our relationships with Christ to the next level. This book is a must-read for any Christian, whether new to the faith or a seasoned traveler."

—**Jamie Jordan**, State Director, South Carolina Christian Chamber of Commerce (C3)

"Mike LaPierre's book, *God's Gift of Imagination*, is a collection of essays from a man with a varied spectrum of life experiences—including professional sports, business management, and church leadership training. It is this wealth of life opportunities that Mike draws from to give the reader some timely and practical thoughts as to how we can use everything God has written in our life story to bring glory to God! He challenges us to live "above" the world and to dedicate ourselves to a purpose that is greater than our personal agendas. You will be blessed, informed, and challenged through the careful reading of this book!"

> —**Pastor John Monroe**, Senior Pastor, Faith Baptist Church (Taylors, South Carolina)

"This book will challenge you to think critically about where you are in your faith walk and how to put that faith into action as a Christian leader. It is full of great insight, wisdom, and biblical truth to help you understand and lead in today's ever-evolving, post-Christian society."

> —**Steven Nail**, Dean of Business School, Anderson University

"Michael LaPierre is a deep Christian thinker, as it were, an apologist. He has thought out many Scriptural principles. He has 'loaded us down' and keeps pointing us to the truth with mountains of verses of Scripture. He exposes the liberal, ungodly, and left-wing forces bent on the destruction of Christianity. If you want to sharpen your mind and deepen your walk with the Lord, read *God's Gift of Imagination*."

> —**Jim Phillips**, Former Pastor for 42 years and Stewardship and Missions Evangelist for 20 years

"In baseball terms, the themes of *God's Gift of Imagination* would include first, a biblical and historical trek that is foundational for developing godly leaders. The path to second base included autobiographical and experiential material that was engaging. Rounding second and heading to third covered analytical and practical data that, if applied, would be life-changing. Waving the reader home, the book is theological, doxological, and refreshingly and conservatively safe. Get a hot dog and a Coke, and enjoy the read!"

> —**Pastor William Senn**, Senior Pastor, Tri-City Baptist Church

"Mike LaPierre has assembled a pithy collection of essays that drill down on some of the most compelling spiritual issues faced by both new and older Christians alike. Drawing upon what he has learned in his personal life and business experiences (he has "been there and done that"), LaPierre clearly communicates the need for an urgent examination of the balance between Biblical faith and the secular influences of contemporary life. Anyone who reads this book should be stirred up to vigilance and a closer walk with God!"

> —**Dr. Stephen Preacher**, Dean, Benson School of Business, Southern Wesleyan University

"Mike LaPierre offers us another thought-provoking review of his leadership principles wrapped in anecdotal stories and biblical allusions that will remind Christians of the practical and imaginative ways that God communicates to us and through us. The format of this book lends itself to reading straight through, or better, a chapter at a time. It would serve as a daily devotional book if the reader would take time to reflect and apply its lessons to his life. May *God's Gift of Imagination* find a broad readership and bring blessing and growth to many."

> —**Dr. John C. Vaughn**

"A graduating future leader once said that the most important outcome of her Christian college experience was this: 'I've learned to take everything I hear, read, and see … and compare it to the Truth.' In this book of essays, Michael LaPierre reminds Christian leaders that God has given us the freedom and ability to imagine without limits, and yet experience the incomparable joy and fulfillment that comes from bringing 'every thought captive to the obedience of Christ' in all realms of life as we seek to love God with both mind and heart."

> —**Dr. Evans Whitaker**, President, Anderson University

"Mike LaPierre has already shown in his first book a desire to point people toward a biblical worldview—especially in practical leadership. This book continues that effort but on an even more practical level. In this work, Mike attempts to 'stir believers to take a position on the issues and shout them from the rooftops.' He exposes the need to identify and take action, and he does it with a solid biblical foundation."

> —**Pastor Douglas Wright**, Senior Pastor, Keystone Baptist
> Church (Berryville, Virginia)

"Each chapter of *God's Gift of Imagination* catapults the reader to a character-building, faith-challenging journey framed by powerful Scripture and inspirational perspectives on how Christian leaders can build influence and impact the world!"

> —**Dr. Todd S. Voss**, President, Southern Wesleyan University

GOD'S GIFT *of* IMAGINATION

STIRRING *the* STEW *with* CHRISTIAN ESSAYS

MICHAEL J. LAPIERRE

HIGH BRIDGE BOOKS
HOUSTON

CONTENTS

About the Author

Michael James LaPierre is a Brown University graduate with Bachelor of Arts degrees in both Organizational Behavior and Management and Political Science. He holds a Master of Business Administration degree from Clemson University with a focus on Entrepreneurship and Innovation. He is an author, motivational speaker, guest lecturer, and founder and current President of *Christian Leadership Worldview International, LLC* (clwi.org).

A former professional baseball player, his executive experiences over the past 30 years include VP of Sales, Director of Sales & Marketing, global strategist, entrepreneur, church servant/deacon, and community leader. His diverse executive background and nonprofit experiences have allowed him to gain a comprehensive understanding of the principles of leadership development. Those broad experiences include leadership positions on management teams in companies such as UPS, Arnold Industries, Lily Transportation, and Roadway Express.

With nonprofit, for-profit, ministerial, and athletic experiences as a backdrop, Michael has the proven ability to capture the essence and fundamentals of leadership training and development. He then relates those varied experiences in a communication style that is motivational, powerful, and relevant to today's employees, students, and organizational leaders.

Mike and his wife, Calie, have been married for more than 34 years. They have three adult children: Ryan, Kyle, and Lauren. They have also been blessed with four grandchildren: Emma, Julia, Cooper, and Tanner. Mike and Calie reside in Pickens, South Carolina.

To contact Mike about speaking at your next leadership event and/or conducting a leadership conference/seminar, you can reach him via the following:

mikelapi@gmail.com
mike@clwi.org
www.clwi.org

But sanctify the Lord God in your hearts: and be ready always to give an answer to every man that asketh you a reason of the hope that is in you with meekness and fear:

—1 PETER 3:5

But to do good and to communicate forget not: for with such sacrifices God is well pleased.

—HEBREWS 13:16

Finally, brethren, whatsoever things are true, whatsoever things are honest, whatsoever things are just, whatsoever things are pure, whatsoever things are lovely, whatsoever things are of good report; if there be any virtue, and if there be any praise, think on these things.

—PHILIPPIANS 4:8

ORGANIZATIONAL AFFILIATIONS

- Christian Leadership Worldview Int'l, Founder/President
- SC Christian Chamber of Commerce, Team Director
- Clemson Chamber of Commerce, Member
- Pickens County Cattlemen's Association, Member
- Toastmasters International, Member
- Advance USA, Ambassador
- Faith Baptist Church (Mentor, College and Career)
- Christian Business Men Connection (CBMC), Member
- Heritage Foundation, Member
- NRA, Member

This book is dedicated to our grandchildren.

Emma
Julia
Cooper
Tanner
Unknown(s)

INTRODUCTION

AT NO TIME IN American history have Christian men and women been more exposed to the magnitude of information that they now experience. It comes at us from all directions through a multitude of channels, dispensing ideas and thoughts that are either appealing or appalling to the senses. Stated another way, the messaging we are receiving from the world is either in line with the Word of God and supports a *Christian leadership worldview* or is opposed to the things of God and supports a cultural understanding of the world in which we live.

We are deceiving ourselves if we think we can have it both ways. The things we allow to seep into our lives have a direct bearing on the condition of our hearts and who we become. The apprehension and rationalization of those concepts help shape our earthly existence and will do much to determine our spiritual influences for His Kingdom. It is naïve to suggest that one can be exposed to the reasoning and theoretical landscape of anti-God sentiment without being burned by the excessive and overwhelming forces of its nature.

As we will discuss in chapter three, our Christian character is shaped in every respect by the trials, afflictions, and life experiences we receive from God, Satan, culture, family, and our minds (the old man within). We know that both God and Christian family members have our best interests at heart. Each wants us to grow in the nurture and admonition of the Lord and become an image of Jesus Christ.

Unfortunately, the other three realms (Satan, the culture, and our minds) have entirely different underlying motives. They want to subject us and the way we perceive the world, process information, and conduct ourselves to the bondage of incorrect spiritual discernment and action. Simply put, they want to lure us in and condition our minds to the platitudes of cultural understanding. The culture would call it being "woke" and in agreement with the cultural norms of the day.

This book will help Christians think about one of the greatest gifts God has given to mankind—the gift of imagination. We must use our brains by thinking critically through every minute detail of all the information that comes our way. Every idea, every thought, and every position that the world presupposes must be examined from a *Christian leadership worldview*. We should learn to take well-thought-out positions on all the issues facing Christians today, leaving no stone unturned.

Beyond this, Christians should also go to great and extraordinary lengths to become master communicators (chapter 13) for the glory of God. Possessing great thoughts and ideas does nothing to impact God's Kingdom if one is not willing to communicate and celebrate the ideation of those little nuggets of Christian thought. Whether through public speaking, writing, or in one-on-one engagements, we must become proficient and persuasive at heralding Bible opinions on what we believe and why we believe them. The articulation of those nuggets will have the impact that Christ desires.

My specific role in all of this and the purpose of this book is to try to stir believers to take positions on the issues and shout them from the rooftops. The best way for me to do that is to share an illustration that combines the delicacies of "lobster stew" (a.k.a. lobsta stew) and the awesome power of the Word of God!

You have probably guessed by now that I am a big fan of lobster stew. I grew up on the coast of Maine, and there is nothing better than large chunks of lobster meat in a thick creamy broth. Yum! In the state of Maine, making lobster stew has become an art form. First, one needs to pick out just the right sized kettle. The bigger, the better in my estimation, as it will create lots of lefto-vers. Next, selecting the ideal wooden spoon for stirring is of vital importance. Finally, you must decide if it will be on an open fire or on the stove. For my dollar, cooking the stew outside on the open fire and letting the salty, fresh air of Maine permeate its fla-vors is the best approach.

Then, there is the all-important ladle. Getting the stew from kettle to plate simply warms the heart. Once again, I opt for the biggest ladle possible since the two-pound lobsters yield impres-sive chunks of lobster meat. Part of the lobster stew experience is watching the lobster stew being ladled into your bowl.

Now, let's talk about all the ingredients. We have fresh minced chives, freshly ground black pepper, paprika, light cream or half-and-half, butter, chopped onions, and the highly esteemed fresh Maine lobster stock and chunks of meat. Can anyone say the word delightful?

A word of caution. One must be careful and diligent about stirring. The more you know about stirring, the better-tasting your recipe will be. A continuous, frequent, or slow stir makes all the difference in the world as you begin to "set up" the con-sistency and flavor of the stew. In our case, since we want to thicken the creamy broth, a continuous stir is important as you slowly and deliberately pour the cream into the kettle.

Warning! If you let the lobster stew sit too long without stir-ring all the ingredients (including the heavenly lobster meat) the stew might have a burnt flavor or after-taste. That is disastrous! The bottom of the kettle may even burn and/or discolor because of one's inattention to stirring. However, if done correctly, the stirring allows the full flavor of the ingredients to combine, con-tribute to, and complement the overall taste, texture, and con-sistency of the stew. As you can see, stirring is a vital and critical component of making the stew. If you slip up in the stirring department, you are going to have some unhappy campers (in-cluding me).

As I was reading 2 Peter 1:5–13, it dawned on me that we have all the ingredients of an amazing Christian life, or what some may call an amazing Christian stew.

> And beside this, giving all diligence, add to your faith virtue; and to virtue knowledge; And to knowledge temperance; and to temperance patience; and to patience godliness; And to godliness brotherly kindness; and to brotherly kindness charity. For if these things be in you, and abound, they make you that ye shall neither be barren nor unfruitful in the knowledge of our Lord Jesus Christ. But he that lacketh these things is blind, and cannot see afar off, and hath forgotten that he was purged from his old sins. Wherefore the rather, brethren, give diligence to make your calling and election sure: for if ye do these things, ye shall never fall: For so an entrance shall be ministered unto you abundantly into the everlasting kingdom of our Lord and Saviour Jesus Christ. Wherefore I will not be negligent to put you always in remembrance of these things, though ye know them, and be established in the present truth. Yea, I think it meet, as long as I am in this tabernacle, **to stir you up** by putting you in remembrance.
> (2 Pet. 1:5–13)

There is a cascading and progressive nature to each of the virtues and godly character traits listed above (faith, virtue, knowledge, temperance, patience, godliness, kindness, charity) that is soothing to the soul and our spiritual tastes. It's a perfect blend and consistency of attributes that bring forth the ultimate spiritual flavor.

However, what most impressed me in these verses was the fact that Peter was there to **stir them up** (v. 13). He was the vital stirring instrument to help them grow in the grace and love needed to succeed in their Christian walk. Peter understood the inadequacies of our frail human natures. He knew that without the constant reminders of the stirring agent (continuous stir), the people of God could fall prey and, consequently, be left to burn by the forces of darkness.

Peter was there to engage and impact their imaginations and thought processes toward the things of the new dispensation and of Jesus Christ. He was also there to help them disengage from the trappings of cultural indoctrination, which at that time was Judaism and the works of the law. Peter was trying to convince them that their salvation was through Christ and Christ alone. The works of the law have no part in our salvation experience. In today's world, the cultural indoctrination we experience comes from the secular humanist crowd. As stated previously, they are trying to condition our minds through ideas and thoughts that come from a multitude of channels. They want burnt lobster stew.

Satan and his followers want us to forget or become numb to the messages of the righteous stirrers by dumbing us down to the cultural understanding and sympathies of the unsaved. We can't let this happen. We can't let our brothers and sisters in Christ slip and burn. The book of Hebrews supports the necessity of listening to and heeding the direction of those godly influencers that can stir us up to remembrance.

> Therefore we ought to give the more earnest heed to the things which we have heard, lest at any time we should let them slip. For if the word spoken by angels was stedfast, and every transgression and disobedience received a just recompence of reward; How shall we escape, if we neglect so great salvation; which at the first began to be spoken by the Lord, and was confirmed unto us by them that heard him; God also bearing them witness, both with signs and wonders, and with divers miracles, and gifts of the Holy Ghost, according to his own will? (Heb. 2:1–4)

I hope and pray that this book inspires and stirs Christians to new ways of critical thinking on the issues that confront us in our present day. I believe if we use the God-given grammatical, dialectic, and rhetorical skills that he has blessed us with, we can do amazing things to impact our culture and redeem the times. Most of all, I am encouraging Christians to dig in, take positions on the issues, communicate their perspectives, and think with a *Christian leadership worldview*.

1

Following Adoniram

The faithful will endure all attempts of the world to stifle the sacred voices of godly reason and commitment—the Christian way of life.

Down through the ages, Brown University has seen a host of their graduates leave an indelible mark on the people they touch and come into contact with. Posterity will view many of these Brown graduates as men and women of renown, who will take their place in the annals of time as extraordinary visionaries and gifted leaders of the human race.

These graduates have demonstrated an uncompromising determination for dramatically changing the world around them with the corresponding idealism, vision, and passion necessary to set them apart from most students and institutions of higher education and learning. Politicians, scholars, clergy, nonprofits, entrepreneurs, executives, and others have dedicated their lives to making a difference for those who follow. The backgrounds from which these graduates come contain an overwhelming diversity of race, creed, color, thought, and liberty of conscience.

It is within this sacred tradition of diversity at Brown that we peer into the world of fundamental Christianity and view the interconnectedness of two Brown graduates who are centuries removed from one another, but with a similar dream. The concern and desire of both graduates was to be yielded and willing instruments to help score Christ's nature on mankind and to leave their Christian marker on everyone they touch. Yes, the hope and prayer of these Brown graduates was/is that everyone they encounter will repent and ask Christ to be their personal Lord and Savior.

The juxtaposition of the ministries of these two born-again believers is the narrative that will follow. The first is a man of unparalleled genius with enough ambition to set out and try to change the world. The second is an ordinary human being with little intellectual bandwidth or natural ability, who simply hopes to approach the ministry of Christ with enough pragmatism, simplicity, and practicality to reach others in the workplace ... one conversation at a time.

> For our rejoicing is this, the testimony of our conscience, that in simplicity and godly sincerity, not in fleshly wisdom, but by the grace of God, we have had our conversation in the world, and more abundantly to you-ward. (2 Cor. 1:12)

Adoniram Judson was arguably one of the most gifted missionaries ever to step foot on foreign lands from the continent of North America. He was a child prodigy who, at age three, was reading entire chapters of the Bible. His doting father was a well-known and respected clergyman who received his formal theological education and training from Yale and filled several Congregational pulpits around New England during Adoniram's upbringing—all the while making sure that his son knew the extraordinarily high expectations that were being placed on him in the spiritual realm to make him someone that God could greatly use in the future.

His godly mother contributed faithfully and energetically to the oversight of the quality of his education in his early childhood years. She was the perfect homemaker, school administrator, thoughtful intellect, and disciplinarian who oversaw his rigorous studies to make sure he was living up to all those high ministry expectations and beyond.

Using his mother's early home school educational training as a springboard, he soon flourished under the tutelage of other institutions of higher education, which included both the Master Dodge School and a school of navigation headed up by Captain Morton. In his early teens Adoniram begin to study and master multiple languages, to the delight of his father (Adoniram Sr.) and his mother (Abigail), while showing an unparalleled aptitude for problem solving and mathematical theory. He had the perfect home environment from which to grow and prosper in his studies.

> As every man hath received the gift, even so minister the same one to another, as good stewards of the manifold grace of God. (1 Pet. 4:10)

Neither Mr. and Mrs. Judson were shy about communicating how much they expected of him. They were sure to frequently tell him that God would use him in unimaginable ways. He should prepare himself to be used like another Massachusetts native who lived in the local vicinity, John Adams. Adams just happened to become President of the United States during Adoniram's formative years. What an impact that must have made on the young and impressionable mind.

Fortunately, Adoniram relished the intellectual stimulation associated with the demands of higher education and learning. He developed an insatiable appetite to be the best that he could be and was driven to strive for notoriety and success. It was in this context, six days after his 16th birthday, that he entered Brown University (the name was changed to Brown shortly after his arrival to Providence, Rhode Island) to take both his intellectual pursuits and ambition out for a spin among his peers in what was considered one of the finest institutions of higher education in the country.

> But the manifestation of the Spirit is given to every man to profit withal. (1 Cor. 12:7)

Well, for those who have any knowledge of his Brown University experience, the case could be made that he experienced both the "thrill of victory and the agony of defeat," like many college students navigating their way as young adults. The thrill of victory came in the intellectual sphere when he entered Brown University as a sophomore (testing and placing out of his freshman year); surrounded himself with a core group of friends who had many of the same talents and drive; and could ultimately challenge him to think above and beyond what was ordinary, simplistic, and customary.

He ended up being the valedictorian at Brown, to the delight of his parents and himself. However, the agony of defeat came when his ambition outpaced his desire to serve a holy and righteous God. He got so caught up in his success and ambition to be someone larger than life and to make a legacy-leaving difference that he lost the true magnet-north of his spiritual compass.

Adoniram experienced a season of life while at Brown that contradicted his Christian upbringing. He decided to flirt with the intellectual construct, stimulation, and rationalism of a deist worldview while disavowing every doctrinal truth he had been taught by his parents from the Word of God. He wanted to be his own man and do his own thing while charting a course in life and in society that would bring him fame, fortune, and notoriety. And, of course, because of his high-minded thinking, he must be right!

It was a period in his life (graduating from Brown at the ripe old age of 19) where he was trying to figure it all out. He wrote and published a couple of math textbooks, tried his hand at acting down in the New York City theatre scene, started a small school, and took on odd-jobs tutoring and mentoring to see him through.

However, deep down inside, none of it was good enough. The things he was involved in still did not fulfill the desires and lusts of his heart. He wanted to be a person of prominence. Adoniram wanted to be a household name. Enter a longsuffering, merciful, and sovereign God:

> Remember not the sins of my youth, nor my transgressions: according to thy mercy remember thou me for thy goodness' sake, O Lord. (Ps. 25:7)

During this time period in Adoniram's life, a couple of key significant events providentially occurred that set the course for his future. First, while on his way back from his New York City acting tour, he had a chance meeting with his best friend from Brown (Jacob Eames of Belfast, Maine) that convicted and challenged his spiritual beliefs and doctrine to the core.

While riding back through a small town in Western Massachusetts from New York City, he decided on a brief stay at an inn for some much-needed rest. However, the inn was full except for one half of a room with a very sick man. The inn keeper indicated that he could section off part of the room for him if Adoniram agreed that it was an acceptable accommodation. He took the room. When checking out of the room the next morning, he found out that the young man who had passed away in the night was his best friend (Jacob Eames) while attending Brown. It was a devastating shock and a wake-up call.

It was quite impossible for Adoniram to see this circumstance as a "chance" meeting. What was God trying to show him through this event? This providential encounter sent his mind reeling about the eternal destiny of his deist friend. What if they had been wrong back at Brown about the principles and doctrine of deism? What if Jesus Christ alone was the only way to heaven? Second, Adoniram was introduced to a couple of Bible-believing "fundamentalists" that were teaching at the Andover Theological

Seminary. They could match wits with Adoniram on an equal basis, argument for argument, debate for debate. They encouraged
him to come to Andover and work out his beliefs with no preconceived worldview. They encouraged him to search the Scriptures
and allow the Spirit of God to lead him in the paths that the Lord
above would have for him. He enrolled at Andover Theological
Seminary at the age of 20. He eventually made the decision to forsake his "deist" leanings and embrace his Lord and Savior Jesus
Christ.

> For whosoever shall call upon the name of the Lord
> shall be saved. (Rom. 10:13)

With the turmoil and confusion of his eternal and doctrinal
paths now put to rest, he continued to struggle with all the pride
that drove both his ambition and heightened sense of self-worth.
The thought that he (not Christ) could impact the world continued to drive him forward. It was also during his time at Andover
that Adoniram found the perfect solution to solve all his earthly
desires. He would enter the mission field as the first missionary
from North American; go to the country of Burma where there
was a desperate need to translate the Bible into the Burmese language; and solve all the family obligations of serving the Lord and
making a difference! And while it would not be the notoriety and
fame that his family had in mind for him, it was such a noble and
worthy spiritual cause that it would be impossible for them to
present any justifiable argument against the heavenly pursuit.

> Trust in the Lord with all thine heart; and lean not
> unto thine own understanding. In all thy ways
> acknowledge him, and he shall direct thy paths.
> (Prov. 3:5–6)

The rest of Adoniram's story is filled with inconceivable life
events of both joy and heartbreak. The joyous occasions took place

when new converts were slowly made; when concentrated periods of Bible translation into the Burmese language occurred; periods of excellent health existed; children were being born; and experiencing the joy of ministry with the godly spouse(s) that was given him.

However, he also suffered much heartache, pain, and suffering while on the mission field in Burma and occasionally in the country of India. He lost two wives and several children to disease and sickness; was thrown into prison and tortured; suffered agonizing periods of poor health and depression; and made little headway in establishing a missionary beachhead that would be sustainable in the country of Burma in the long-term. The spreading of the gospel message was a slow and arduous process as a result of the government's unwillingness to let foreign missionaries gain any real inroads.

We can now look back in history and see how God was orchestrating the events in Burma in His timing while exercising some of the important lessons of life that Adoniram needed for spiritual growth—his total reliance on the Lord for doing the work of missions and translating the language, and removing all notions of high-minded thinking and overvalued self-worth. Over time, the circumstances and life events taught him that God's thoughts and ways were much higher than man's thoughts and ways.

In the end, God used Adoniram in unimaginable ways. He completed both the Burmese Bible translation and a dictionary for the language. He also saw God make significant inroads in Burma that would have lasting spiritual impact for decades and centuries to come. God accomplished many wonderful and glorious things in Burma; however, it was all done on his timetable.[1]

> For as the heavens are higher than the earth, so are my ways higher than your ways, and my thoughts than your thoughts. (Isa. 55:9)

Almost 200 years later, God called another Brown graduate (class of 1983) in the Baptist tradition to leave Christ's marker on various parts of the world. This graduate is content with using the gifts he has been given to impact others on a much smaller scale but desires to lead and have an impact nonetheless. There are no thoughts of grandeur, prominence, or feeding an overactive ambition for greatness. No, there is only the dream of impacting others for Christ within the sphere of his influence and with the credentials/spiritual gifts that the Creator of this world has endowed him with.

While there is little greatness or things that others could recommend as unique for this graduate, he hopes and prays that he will be used. Simply put, he is a sinner saved by the grace of God. Outside of Jesus Christ, there is nothing exemplary for this Christian in his natural state. This ordinary person must rely totally on God's grace and direction for His will to be accomplished. What follows is a first-person account of the providential orchestration of the life events of a second Brown alumni that point to a Savior.

The law of the LORD is perfect, converting the soul: the testimony of the LORD is sure, making wise the simple. (Ps. 19:7)

Growing up in rural Maine certainly presented some difficult challenges. Looking back, it is evident that God was preparing me for His service. He was refining me in a way that was tailor-made for my specific Christian journey that lay ahead. I was shy, self-conscious, and painfully aware that my intellectual capabilities were limited. It didn't take much for me to get totally embarrassed and turn beet red at the drop of a hat.

My mom and dad were relatively poor, not being able to afford any of the extravagances of life. However, we always had food on the table, clothes on our backs, and a roof over our heads! My parents wanted much more for their children than they were blessed with. They provided for us the best way they knew how.

Our mother was a stay-at-home mom for most of my upbringing (there were periods of employment when times were tough), while dad held various deputy sheriff and town constable positions in Southern Maine.

While we called ourselves Christians, our dedication to church and the fruits of our spiritual labor were lacking or nonexistent during the first 23 years of my life. We were relatively poor, unchurched, of French descent, without higher education (I was the first in our family to attend college), who were satisfied with being able to struggle and survive.

If not satisfied, my parents had a hard time knowing just how to pull themselves out of their circumstances. There was little-to-no driving ambition to achieve great things—just love for their children and hopes that they would one day grow to be adults they could be proud of. For their love, encouragement, and protection, I am most grateful. For me, the one added "bonus" to all of this was my abnormal appearance. Thick glasses and great big buck teeth had to be the envy of all my friends, didn't it? Well, of course not. The ridicule, bullying, and sarcastic comments were never-ending up through the sixth-grade. I wasn't pleasant to look at and I knew it. My peers reminded me on a continual basis that I was different and not quite like them. Through all the difficulties of early childhood, God saw fit to bless me with a few small character traits, gifts, and advantages that he would use for His glory.

> But God hath chosen the foolish things of the world
> to confound the wise; and God hath chosen the weak
> things of the world to confound the things which are
> mighty; (1 Cor. 1:27)

First, I loved to compete and win. Second, I was passionate about athletics. When you combine these two elements, there is the potential for getting a lot of things accomplished. The more I was made fun of, the harder I competed on the court and playing fields. The more my peers pointed out my inadequacies, the more I was determined to compete and win in the athletic realm to show that I should be valued and appreciated. I was driven to be the best athlete possible.

Now enter Brown University. How could a person with average intelligence get into an Ivy League School you ask? How could someone with less than a 3.0 GPA in high school with SAT scores south of 1000 get in an elite university? By a divine orchestration and a providential roadmap. God had some important work for me to do later in life. He knew that He wanted me to proclaim His name to various parts of the world and made sure that He laid the pathway to achieve His perfect will in my life!

It just so happened that the baseball coach at Brown drove to my high school (Bonny Eagle High School in West Buxton, Maine) and showed up at one of my basketball practices. Yes, I did say basketball practice. I had one of the best practices of my entire life. Some might even say that I dominated the practice. That day I noticed a man in the stands but was unaware that he was a baseball coach from Brown on a recruiting trip. After the practice, he drove me home and asked if I was interested in attending Brown University. I immediately showed all my cards (innocence and naivety) and mentioned that I had never heard of Brown before. Where was it located? What was it all about? Was the baseball team any good? Would I be starting? That was all I was interested in at the time.

Well, one week later and as a result of that one basketball practice, the baseball coached called me and mentioned that I was going to be his #1 baseball recruit! How did he even know that I could play baseball, I wondered? Later, I found out that he talked to my basketball coach who said a few flattering things about my desire to compete and win. I was so excited about the prospect of playing baseball at a school that seemed genuinely interested in me and my baseball talents! However, there was still that little challenge of convincing the university's admission board that if accepted, I would be able to handle the academic challenges that lay ahead. I can't blame them for worrying about letting someone into their university who had demonstrated so little aptitude for higher education.

I then proceeded, in typical form, to botch my admissions essay and got it returned to me with a note from my coach. Coach mentioned that I should take the essay very seriously and that I should put a compelling story together of why I would be a good fit at Brown University. I changed a few sentences around, sent it back in and waited for a response. I was being recruited by a few other schools for baseball at the time (University of Vermont and Rollins College) and didn't really care. In the meantime, while waiting for a response, I began to investigate what the school was all about. I found out that it was an Ivy League School. So what? What does that mean? It had rigorous academic standards. Most of the students were exceptionally bright people. Then the light went on and I realized that I might be in trouble if I went there! I was a lousy student who didn't apply myself (i.e., work hard) and would be potentially attending a challenging university.

A few months later, I was notified that I was accepted. My friends, teachers, and other peers at my high school could not believe it! They were beside themselves. They all knew my study habits and my class ranking and could not believe that Brown had let me into their quality university. After much agonizing and contemplation about my college decision, I decided to attend Brown University. Once at Brown, I learned early on what it would take to survive. It was going to take a determination and competitive spirit like no other I have ever experienced.

In the end I was privileged to have completed both Political Science and Organizational Behavior & Management degrees while attending the university. It certainly was not a result of my intellect. It was more a result of the God-given competitive spirit I was blessed with. I believe that the Creator of this world orchestrated my four years at Brown. There were also multiple occasions while at Brown where Christians witnessed to me about my need for the Lord. Several of them willingly shared the good news of the gospel with me. The seeds were being sown and God was charting an unimaginable path in my life. I was still a long way from accepting Christ as my Savior.

Enter baseball. I had an absolute blast playing baseball during my college years. I took it very seriously. I spent hours upon hours in the weight room and batting cage. I was determined to compete at the highest levels in college and beyond. I made honorable mention my freshman year and hit .333, and I was blessed with First Team All-New England and First Team All-Ivy League Honors in my junior year. Coach Stenhouse told me that I could potentially be a top 10 pick in the amateur baseball draft in June 1982.

Then the unthinkable happened. I remember like it was yesterday. We were playing a game at Cornell University on a cold, blistery day in April 1982. I reached first base on an infield hit and then immediately stole second base on the very next pitch. Two pitches later, I was on my way to third base attempting to steal third. Three quarters of the way there, I felt a rip in my hamstring. I was devastated. There were still two weeks in the season with a bunch of games left, and I had to play injured with a ripped hammy. The results were pathetic. I just could not get around on the ball at the plate like I needed to. I could barely make it down the base paths.

My average dropped from .424 to .376 by the end of my junior year. A wonderful average in many respects, but not where I wanted to end up. In the ensuing All-Star game that year, I again tried to play with the injury. My coach convinced me to play, and it was disastrous. I re-injured my hamstring and struck out three times. The professional baseball scouts backed way off. They wanted to see how the hamstring would react to therapy and whether the base stealing ability and speed would still be there the following year. They wanted to see me play again in my senior year and "passed" on drafting me as a junior.

My world was turned upside down. I was angry, bitter, resentful, and wanted to quit baseball. I felt like my chances to play professionally were all but gone. Why this injury? Why me? Why now? Once again, looking back, I can clearly see that it was part of God's plan. He was simply slowing down my enthusiasm for the game of baseball a little. The Lord was trying to recalibrate my sensitivities to a life beyond baseball.

But then the unthinkable happened. I was called by the Montreal Expos baseball team on a fateful day in June 1983 and was asked to sign a professional baseball contract. I could never quite figure out why the Expos would express any interest in me (outside of God's divine plan) since my senior year was once again injury plagued with little productivity. I hit .333 again with limited at bats. I re-injured my hamstring for the fourth or fifth time and struggled to contribute to the team's success.

I had all but given up on the hopes and dreams of playing professionally, but the phone call came from the Expos just the same, and I was on cloud nine. After the phone call, I went into my bedroom and cried like a baby. While still unsaved at the time, I knelt by my bedside and thanked God for the opportunity to play professional baseball. After an abbreviated spring training, it was off to Calgary, Alberta, Canada and the Calgary Expos for my very first season of Class A baseball (rookie league). It was a dream that finally came true! Wow!

On the baseball front, things didn't go so well. My one and only season with the Expos seemed to be a replay of my senior year at Brown. I suffered one injury after another, with little playing time as a result. It was frustrating. However, by the end of that first season, baseball success just didn't matter to me anymore. The passion and desire to climb the minor league ladder to reach the major leagues was gone.

While I had an additional opportunity to continue my minor league journey, God saw fit to replace my baseball passion with more important spiritual interests and desires. Quite frankly, it was the most important period of my life. A fellow Calgary Expos teammate and Christian befriended me during the season. We

spent a lot of time together. He had a Christian joy and counte-
nance that was overflowing and exuded a Christlike character.
Van Samples was a young believer who was a bold witness for
Christ and someone who walked the talk. I realized that I wanted
and needed the joy he had in his life. Van repeatedly told me of
my need for a Savior and gave me the clear gospel message of
Christ. He mentioned that I needed to repent, ask forgiveness for
my sins, and ask Christ to save me and rule in my life.

> For all have sinned, and come short of the glory of
> God. (Rom. 3:23)

It was the defining moment in my life that I will cherish
through eternity. One night after a baseball game while playing
in Calgary, I put on my jogging cloths and went out for a run. I
ended up back at the baseball diamond where we had just played
an hour before. There was no one around and all the lights for the
field were still turned on. I jumped the fence and walked out into
centerfield. It was there that I got down on my knees and received
Jesus Christ as my Savior. That defining moment of truth was a
springboard to the rest of my life. I got married to a wonderful
Christian woman, had three children and four grandchildren (so
far), and have been married for 34 years. God also allowed me to
spend the next 33 years in Corporate America leading sales teams
and impacting global strategy at the highest levels. A VP of Sales,
Director of Sales and Marketing, and Global Sales Strategist were
just a few of the stops along the way (godly training opportunities) to condition me for His service in the years ahead.

> And unto man he said, behold, the fear of the Lord,
> that is wisdom; and to depart from evil is understand-
> ing. (Job 28:28)

It is within the confines and limitations of any natural ability
that God has allowed this second Brown University graduate to

found *Christian Leadership Worldview International* (CLWI). It was simply a divine orchestration from above with the experiences of life necessary to be able to make a difference in this world for Christ. There is no other possible way to catalog my life events. This organization is a 501(c)(3) nonprofit that impacts others for Christ with a leadership training and development focus and format.

The CLWI organization travels the globe conducting leadership training and development from a biblical perspective. The Christian training offered is geared for a marketplace understanding. As Christians, how do we respond to the workplace? What is the playing field like? How do we navigate our various encounters and moments of truth? What is our authority to lead in the workplace, and where does it come from? As Christians, if we are considered both royal priests and kings at the point of conversion, where do our responsibilities begin and end as we live out our faith each day "outside" of the four walls of a church building? How can we bring glory to God in a workplace environment? These questions and more set the stage for the burden of the CLWI ministry. We hope to bring an explosion of awareness to both believers and non-believers about what the Bible has to say about our responsibilities while at work — a responsibility so great that it must be communicated to the world.

> And hast made us unto our God kings and priests:
> and we shall reign on the earth. (Rev. 5:10)

There remains another unique and providential connection between the two Brown University graduates above. Adoniram Judson, the Christian Leadership Worldview International ministry, and the countries of India and Burma are intertwined and connected in heavenly places. The CLWI ministry has recently been blessed to have participated in the First Annual Good News

360 Leadership Conference in India. We were able to teach leadership seminars and preach God's Word to over 800 Indian Christians!

The executive coordinator of the Good News 360 Conference is Billy Judson. Yes, his last name is representative of Adoniram Judson, who had a tremendous impact on his family's lineage and history. Generations ago, Billy Judson's ancestors were saved under Adoniram Judson's missionary endeavors. Some of his family members even went back to the field in Burma as missionaries to teach and preach the gospel message of Christ. A native of India, Billy Judson feels compelled to reach his Indian countrymen for Christ. What a joy it was for this Brown graduate and the CLWI ministry to go to the country of India and contribute much the same way Adoniram did centuries earlier. While Adoniram's primary burden was for the country of Burma, he was also a great blessing to the country of India as well.

> Go ye therefore, and teach all nations, baptizing them in the name of the Father, and of the Son, and of the Holy Ghost: Teaching them to observe all things whatsoever I have commanded you: and, lo, I am with you always, even unto the end of the world. (Matt. 28:19–20)

Please pray that the CLWI ministry can impact others for Christ. Pray that God would open the doors around the world for us to teach and preach Christian leadership principles in the workplace. We do not want notoriety, fame, or accolades. We simply want to be remembered as Christians who were willing to use their spiritual gifts to the fullest extent, Christians who were not willing to sit in the stands of life but were willing to step out and get involved. Praise God for all He has done and will be doing in the future. We only desire to hear those wonderful words of praise from God when we meet Him in heaven.

His lord said unto him, Well done, good and faithful servant; thou hast been faithful over a few things, I will make thee ruler over many things: enter thou into the joy of thy lord. (Matt. 25:23)

---

[1] Courtney Anderson, *The Life of Adoniram Judson, To the Golden Shores,* (Published by Judson Press, 1987).

2

How Is Your Spiritual Well-Being?

Life is the existence of God in us; the demonstration of
God through us; and the love of God to us.

I RECENTLY HAD THE pleasure of attending a meeting at a local chapter of an organization designed to help improve one's public speaking and communication abilities. The main presenter discussed a topic that made me seriously contemplate the underlying message. The speech clearly had an impact on my sensibilities and made me think beyond the generalities of the message. The topic was titled, "Foundations." As I boiled down the main premise of the message, it occurred to me that the speaker was a Christian who challenged us to consider the foundations of life and whether we are relying on the sands of humanity or the solid rock of everlasting hope (Jesus Christ). Do we believe in the lies of this world or the truth of God's Word? It was a brilliant, timely (Christmas season), and inspiring message that stirred me to think more broadly about my own spiritual foundation and where in that continuum of progressive sanctification I am currently stationed. In other words, "How far have I progressed in my walk with the Lord?" The remaining portion of this chapter is dedicated to an expansion of the preceding topical "foundation" for self-examination, reflection, and critical thinking.

When we consider those much-sought-after words upon entering heaven's glory, "Well done thy good and faithful servant," it strikes me that there are two primary points of their construction. First, there is the completion of the service we have rendered for the glory of God through our many Christian vocations. We are being acknowledged for our passion, dedication, and diligence to the works we have undertaken here on earth for the King of kings and Lord of lords.

Our Maker is commenting on our actions, thoughts, words, and motivations. The one true God—who is omniscient (all knowing), omnipresent (everywhere at all times), omnipotent (all powerful), and immutable (never changing)—wants to commend our service to His kingdom. Second, it is also evident that our faithfulness is being divinely acknowledged as a key building block to the successful foundation of Christian living. That faithfulness is because of the trust and faith we have placed in Jesus Christ.

But two questions must be asked. First, "How do we get there?" Second, "What fundamental drivers does the Holy Spirit use to help us along our way as ambassadors and sojourners here on earth?" The Lord has provided two key inspired means which the Spirit of God uses to sanctify us and get us ready for His glory. We can unshakably believe in the absolute authority of His Word (faith) and walk by faith and not by sight (2 Cor. 5:7). The Bible tells us, "Now faith is the substance of things hoped for, and the evidence of things not seen (Heb. 11:1)." We can also show our love to Him through our works. He wants ownership of our hearts through obedience to His Word. That obedience, by its very nature, requires us to thoughtfully consider our good works toward God and for the benefit of others.

My son, give me thine heart and let thine eyes observe my ways. (Prov. 23:26)

Commit thy works unto the Lord and thy thoughts
will be established. (Prov. 16:3)

The Bible clearly supports the eternal significance of faith and
the subsequent works derived from a spirit of love as we yield to
His holy and righteous nature. While we are justified by faith and
faith alone, the outpouring of our love toward Him will be made
manifest in our obedience to His Word through our works.

Therefore we conclude that a man is justified by faith
without the deeds of the law. (Rom. 3:28)

Even so faith, if it hath not works, is dead, being
alone. (Jas. 2:17)

But be ye doers of the word, and not hearers only, deceiving your own selves. (Jas. 1:22)

It can also be deduced that our station in life (spiritual well-
being) is directly tied to the degree in which we genuinely demonstrate both our faith and good works. For the purpose of modeling
our spiritual well-being, let's assume there are only four quadrants in this regard: Q1 (Low Faith – Low Works), Q2 (Low Faith
– High Works), Q3 (High Faith – High Works), Q4 (High Faith –
Low Works). For simplicity purposes, we may even call each of
these quadrants sandboxes. Ideally, each sandbox is a place where
we learn, grow, mature, change, and interact with others. Each
sandbox is a snapshot of one's spiritual progress at a given point
in time—some to the praise of His glory, others to a hope of a
brighter tomorrow or a more sure testimony of faith.

Based on one's spiritual progression, individuals will fall
somewhere in one of the four quadrants. Since this model is only
designed to help us consider and self-examine our current state
of Christian readiness, we can take enormous comfort in the fact
that God's work in our lives is not yet complete. Let's now take a

deeper look into the specific quadrants provided for in this chapter and what the definition of each may mean to our spiritual state of well-being and Christian readiness levels.[1]

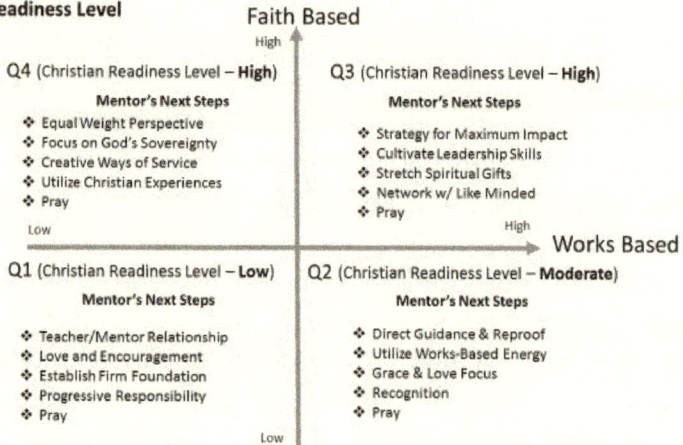

Spiritual Well-Being Model

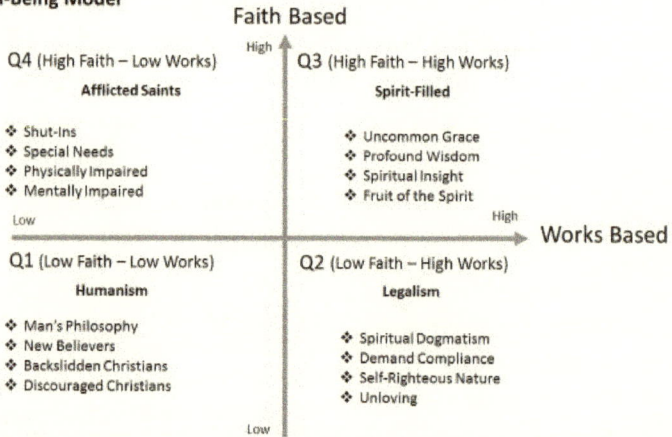

Faith Based

High

Q4 (High Faith – Low Works)

Afflicted Saints

- ❖ Shut-Ins
- ❖ Special Needs
- ❖ Physically Impaired
- ❖ Mentally Impaired

Low

Q3 (High Faith – High Works)

Spirit-Filled

- ❖ Uncommon Grace
- ❖ Profound Wisdom
- ❖ Spiritual Insight
- ❖ Fruit of the Spirit

High

Works Based

Q1 (Low Faith – Low Works)

Humanism

- ❖ Man's Philosophy
- ❖ New Believers
- ❖ Backslidden Christians
- ❖ Discouraged Christians

Q2 (Low Faith – High Works)

Legalism

- ❖ Spiritual Dogmatism
- ❖ Demand Compliance
- ❖ Self-Righteous Nature
- ❖ Unloving

Low

Christian Readiness Level

Faith Based

High

Q4 (Christian Readiness Level – **High**)

Mentor's Next Steps

- ❖ Equal Weight Perspective
- ❖ Focus on God's Sovereignty
- ❖ Creative Ways of Service
- ❖ Utilize Christian Experiences
- ❖ Pray

Low

Q3 (Christian Readiness Level – **High**)

Mentor's Next Steps

- ❖ Strategy for Maximum Impact
- ❖ Cultivate Leadership Skills
- ❖ Stretch Spiritual Gifts
- ❖ Network w/ Like Minded
- ❖ Pray

High

Works Based

Q1 (Christian Readiness Level – **Low**)

Mentor's Next Steps

- ❖ Teacher/Mentor Relationship
- ❖ Love and Encouragement
- ❖ Establish Firm Foundation
- ❖ Progressive Responsibility
- ❖ Pray

Q2 (Christian Readiness Level – **Moderate**)

Mentor's Next Steps

- ❖ Direct Guidance & Reproof
- ❖ Utilize Works-Based Energy
- ❖ Grace & Love Focus
- ❖ Recognition
- ❖ Pray

Low

---

[1] Dr. Paul Hersey, *The Situational LEADER* (USA: Center for Leadership Studies, 1992).

Quadrant #1 (Low Faith – Low Works) – Humanism

Q1 represents those individuals who have contrasting worldviews to those of Christianity; new Christian believers who are just getting started and trying to find their spiritual footing; those who are backslidden in the faith and to the things of the Lord; and born-again believers who are in a state of discouragement.

This first group espouses doctrine and a worldview which are anti-God and are *secular humanist* in nature. This group doesn't know Christ, is "of the world," and places the preeminence of man's "being" and situation in life on his authority, his greatness and ingenuity, and his ultimate ability to use reason, intelligence, and logic to conquer the world's dilemmas and solve their problems. It is essentially enlightenment-period thinking, which credits the intellectual superiority of mankind for moving us forward toward better and more meaningful ends.

The humanist worldviews are informed by their *personal* philosophies of life. Even born-again believers, when making decisions and acting in the flesh, are in danger of contributing to the approbation of philosophical humanism and a secular way of reasoning, thinking, and acting. Just think about the last statement for a moment. When we hastily, impetuously, loftily, or flippantly make decisions in the flesh without walking in the Spirit, seeking godly counsel, and seeking the will of God, they become fleshly and earthly sentiments and passions driven by man's desires, not God's.

In theory, while as Christians we may not knowingly yield in support of the specific tenants of Secular Humanism and its corresponding religion, we indirectly propagate their religious indoctrination at the fringes of society and Christianity itself with man-made decisions and philosophies. The trickle-down and subtlety of our man-made decision-making can have an enormous impact on friends, family, loved ones, and society in general. In essence, we are encroaching the throne of God with this behavior and replacing His will with our own. Some would even go so far as to say that we are trampling and denigrating His throne with this type of behavior.

The second group in Q1 are new believers in Christ who haven't yet learned to express and demonstrate a "living faith" and the obedience (works) needed to help glorify a holy, just, and righteous God. They are brothers and sisters in Christ who made a profession of faith and are at the starting blocks of their individual spiritual marathons, called Christianity. This group desperately needs godly counsel and guidance. They need to be quickly plugged in with mature Christians who can more fully expound the Christian faith and the doctrine of God's grace.

> And the things that thou hast heard of me among many witnesses, the same commit thou to faithful men, who shall be able to teach others also.
> (2 Tim. 2:2)

The third group we will consider in Q1 are those that are backslidden. These individuals may even be lukewarm in their spiritual nature and show no desire toward faith and obedience. The Bible warns us about those who exhibit a backslidden state. Much like their secular humanist counterparts, the backslider is filled with his own ways and devices. The church at Ephesus is symbolic of the Christian who has left their first love:

> Nevertheless, I have somewhat against thee, because thou hast left thy first love. Remember therefore from whence thou are fallen, and repent, and do the first works; or else I will come unto thee quickly, and will remove thy candlestick out of his place, except thou repent. (Rev. 2:4–5)

> The backslider in heart shall be filled with his own ways. (Prov. 14:14)

God also is clear about those in a lukewarm state as described in the book of Revelation to the church of Laodicea. Again, the symbolism here instructs our understanding of His expectations for our lives:

> I know thy works, that thou art neither cold nor hot: I would thou were cold or hot. So then because thou art lukewarm, and neither cold nor hot, I will spit thee out of my mouth. (Rev. 3:15–16)

The last group in Q1 are those who are burdened with discouragement. Their despondency toward the things of God is a result of some major tragedy or life-changing occurrence, and they are reeling from the consequences and effects of those difficult situations. They do not have a willful disregard for the things of the Lord but are either in mourning or shocked by events.

For those of you who find yourself in Q1, regardless of the group that you relate to above, you are in great danger. Yes, even those who made a *profession* of faith must take great care that their profession was real, genuine, and had deep roots. The book of Luke and the parable of the sower helps us further understand the caution with which we must proceed. Remember, God wants our hearts and not mere words with the sheen of formality and religiosity.

Now the parable is this:

> The seed is the Word of God. Those by the wayside are they that hear; then cometh the devil, and taketh away the word out of their hearts, lest they should believe and be saved. They on the rock are they, which, when they hear, receive the word with joy; and these have no root, which for a while believe, and in time of

temptation fall away. And that which fell among thorns are they, which, when they have heard, go forth, and are choked with cares and riches and pleasures of this life, and bring no fruit to perfection. But that on the good ground are they, which in an honest and good heart, having heard the word, keep it, and bring forth fruit with patience. (Luke 8:11–15)

However, if you are currently residing in Q1, take heart. There is great hope for the unsaved if you repent of your sins, turn, and place your faith and trust in the Risen Savior, Jesus Christ! For those new believers just starting out or those who are discouraged, have the faith of a mustard seed and watch God do amazing things through you.

Q1 Christian Readiness Level – Low

Mentor's Next Steps – Guide them with the milk of God's Word to establish a firm foundation. Use the love and encouragement necessary to lift them to new spiritual heights. Challenge them to progressively take on more responsibility for the Kingdom of God. Acknowledge their spiritual progress. Stay close to Q1 members as they develop with a teacher/mentor relationship, incorporating varying levels of accountability. Pray.

Quadrant #2 – (Low Faith – High Works) – Legalism

Q2 represents those individuals who have a high affinity to the works of righteousness and the law but fail to embrace an active obedience to the faith of His Word. The cascading impact of a lack of faith can be overwhelming and a heavy burden to this group.

Q2 can be very deceptive. To the naked eye and by all appearances, this group of individuals is hard at work. However, they go through life simply checking all the boxes of *spiritual dogmatism* by copiously fulfilling and obeying the expectations of the law. This group is enveloped by the nature and works of the law. Intellectually, they understand most of God's promises, principles, and precepts. These born-again Christians can quote chapter and verse and rigidly *demand compliance* with the tenants of God's Word. They have a thirst for sacrificing their time, talents, and finances unto the Lord with little faith. They do so out of obligation, tradition, recognition, and routine; outside of the love and grace provided through a deep and abiding faith in Christ Jesus.

They are extremely busy people. All that they do and all that they have become is through sheer willpower. They have failed to be instructed by an unwavering faith along with God's providence, protection, and divine orchestration needed to help guide them on their Christian journey. They have let the works of obedience to the law crowd out the two most important commandments found in His Word. We should be crushed and humbled by the words of Jesus as He tells us to love God and to love our neighbors:

> And Jesus answered him, The first of all the commandments is, Hear, O Israel; The Lord our God is one Lord: And thou shalt love the Lord thy God with all thy heart, and with all thy soul, and with all thy mind, and with all thy strength; this is the first commandment. And the second is like, namely this, Thou shalt love thy neighbor as thyself. There is none other commandment greater than these. (Mark 12:29–31)

Unfortunately, love is oftentimes a missing part of this group's makeup. They have become so entrenched with a *works-based* and legalistic approach to their faith that they feel helpless when trying to escape the vortex of *legalism*. The depths of legalism can be both confining and restraining. Confining in the sense that this group can feel imprisoned with the chains of mean-spiritedness, inflexibility, dogmatism, and an unloving nature. Restrained in the sense that they are not able to execute and live out one of the most fundamental doctrines of the Christian faith—love.

Q2 participants understand intellectually that they should be walking by faith and loving others, but they have failed to incorporate faith and trust into their everyday standards of living and their walk with Christ. They fail to live the *active obedience* necessary in a faith-based Christianity. As a result, they don't grasp the depth of God's love toward them and consequently *fail to demonstrate their love* toward others. It appears to be a heads-down, process-driven approach to one's faith that wreaks of legalism and an unloving nature. Their ability to yield and submit to the entire authority of God's Word is questionable because they are unwilling to adorn all of the doctrines of God our Savior in everything they do (Titus 2:10).

> And walk in love, as Christ also hath loved us, and
> hath given himself for us an offering and a sacrifice to
> God for a sweet-smelling savour. (Eph. 5:2)

Another potential characteristic of those in Q2 is one of a *self-righteous nature*. They can be quick to censure and point out the deficiencies and sinful nature of others while unwilling to face the immense struggle of sin, iniquity, and pride from their old man within. Some in this quadrant have never met a mote that they did not recognize and quickly point out. To be fair, many of those who appear to be self-righteous in nature may simply have a blind spot that needs to be lovingly exercised by the counsel of God's Word and close Christian friends. Outside of this exception, most of those who are self-righteous are driven by the need to be recognized for their superiority of mind and deed. The origin of their pride can be traced back to the lack of approbation in their early years. They are trying to impress those who had a direct (albeit questionable) influence on their upbringing. Their pride, egocentricity, and ongoing censure of others fills a missing void from their early years. They need to be recognized.

> And why beholdest thou the mote that is in thy brother's eye, but perceivest not the beam that is in thine own eye? (Luke 6:41)

The Q2 individuals have a *weak spiritual foundation* that may look good in the eyes of others or even to themselves. Because they have high energy (works-based), I believe that most of those in Q2 have an acute understanding of their need to deepen and broaden their faith. Internally, they are conflicted because of the need to love other people. They look at the world through the eyes of a Pharisee.

Q2 Christian Readiness Level – Moderate

Mentor's Next Steps – Utilize their works-based energy to push them in another direction. While being full of grace, love, and concern, mentors for those in Q2 may need to exhibit a more direct and tough love approach for legalists. Point out all the wonderful things they are doing for the Lord while cautioning and encouraging them to grasp in total the other half of the story (love). Remember, they are probably aware of their shortcomings in this regard. They just need someone to come along and hold them accountable by giving clear direction, show love and concern, and then get out of the way. Once they are free from the constraining and restraining elements of a legalist vortex, they have the potential to flourish beyond our wildest imaginations. Pray.

Quadrant #3 – (High Faith – High Works) – Spirit-Filled

I have tremendous admiration, awe, and respect for this group of believers. They have learned how to *take refuge* in the shadow of the wings of the Almighty God. They are not tossed about with every wind of doctrine and lead a quiet and *peaceable* existence unto the Lord. Q3 Christians are able to actively live out and obey Romans 11:36:

> For of him, and through him, and to him, are all things: to whom be glory for ever. Amen.

Their words are seasoned with *uncommon grace* that inspires others to reach for the stars and be the best that they can be for the Lord. Everyone wants to be around them; everyone wants to be their friend. Even their enemies are made to be at peace with them. They always seem to say and do the right things at the exact moment needed with a deep and *profound wisdom* that only can come from walking with God. To be in this Christian's presence is a privilege and an honor.

Q3 Christians help impact and mold the spiritual components of the believer's existence while giving little deference to the hay, stubble, and chaff all around them. They guide us with their *spiritual insights*, forethought, and Christian experiences from the lowest valleys to the highest mountaintops. The crosses they carry and bare and the spiritual wounds they have received from above are ever before them.

There is no mistaking these faithful and obedient Christians. They truly are the *salt of the earth*. They exude what absolute truth should look like. Indeed, they represent the most righteous and holy aspects of what it means to be Christian. They have *learned how to love*. They have *learned how to be content*. They have long ago

and willingly left the poisonous shroud of self, humbling themselves at the feet of the master. Their *joy is contagious*. What they
represent is clearly visible to all those they encounter. They are
the living standard of what the beatitudes stand for. They live and
breathe the *fruit of the Spirit*. Our Father in heaven has given them
an unparalleled measure of both faith and works to impact our
culture, and they do so willingly, passionately, and without question. They are truly *blessed from above*. How else are we to describe
these Spirit-filled Christians other than to say that they are walking with God and made in His image? Amen.

Q3 Christian Readiness Level – High

Mentor's Next Steps – Mentors must be mindful of using these
Christian warriors in ways that will have maximum impact on
our culture and reach the masses. In many respects, they are
Christians who should be mentoring other people. God has prepared Q3 Christians for spiritual warfare, and those that offer
counsel to them must go out of their way to make sure their gifts
are being effectively utilized. Their Christian leadership skills
must be nourished and cultivated with the most ardent care and
forethought possible. It is important to continue to stretch the
boundaries of their spiritual gifts. Galatians chapter 5 is extremely
important to these Q3 Christians. Interacting with other Christians who have been given equal measures of faith and obedience
to good works will sharpen these Q3 Christians. Pray.

Quadrant #4 – (High Faith – Low Works) – Afflicted Saints

I also have tremendous admiration, awe, and respect for this
group of believers. The Christian believers in this quadrant have
been given various afflictions that redirect and refocus the exercise of their good works. Many of these believers are high-faith

Q3 Christians whose responsibilities and priorities have been re-directed. To try to understand why God would allow such occur-rences is beyond the scope of this chapter. However, we take great comfort in knowing that "all things work together for good to them that love God, to them who are the called according to his purpose" (Rom. 8:28).

We also understand that their *contributions are no less valued* as part of the body of the church, only different. God uses these individuals in ways that you and I will never understand this side of heaven. They may be afflicted beyond what most people con-sider "normal" health but to say that they are in any way re-stricted in how God uses them would be incorrect. We can say that because we serve a sovereign Lord. They are *perfectly and wonderfully made*. While the multiplicity and types of works may be limited in number, they are in no way limited in impact for the cause of Christ:

> **Shut-Ins** – Many in this category are seasoned saints who have fought the good fight of Christianity but are now afflicted with the blessings of older age. They have great faith. Their ability to express their good works in multiple forums with an extensive range of impact is now slowed by the degradation of the flesh. Conse-quently, they have switched gears and narrowed their works focus to things that they are capable of. What they do is still very meaningful. They may not be out leading the charge anymore but silently and with much gusto praying for those who do. They write letters, send emails, pray, send tracts, and communicate the blessed message of the gospel and the hope that we have in Je-sus. When they are with family and friends, they have great influence. Their Christian legacies and their works of old have not gone unnoticed, leaving a distinct and well-traveled trail of faith and works. We salute and honor them for their renewed but different service unto

the Lord. Matthew Henry had a quote in his commentary on the Bible that I believe, in some instances, describes the position in which some faithful shut-ins find themselves. He said, "We must be God's waiting servants when we can no longer be his working servants."

Special Needs – Their happiness, enthusiasm, blind faith, and uniqueness is overflowing and impactful to those they encounter. With childlike faith, they can share the love of Jesus in places where others can't. We are amazed and stand in awe of how the Lord uses them to accomplish His purposes. They have impact. They are a blessing from above.

Physically and Mentally Impaired – God also greatly uses those who struggle with physical and mental health issues. While their sphere of influence may be curtailed in many instances, God still uses them in mighty ways for His Kingdom. Those who are completely immobile, stricken with disease, or those who have debilitating periods of depression first come to mind. While those in Q4 have great faith, their works are limited to specific functions. As I have stated previously, they, too, are no less valued but critical to the proper functioning of the local body of believers, His church.

Q4 Christian Readiness Level – High

Mentor's Next Steps – Those Christians in Q4 who exhibit high faith and who may experience some type of limiting affliction (but perfect) must be encouraged to look at their spiritual "sandbox" with equal weight. By human measure and understanding (not God's), their opportunities may be limited and confined in scope; therefore, mentors must go to great lengths to convince them of the importance of what they do. Their specific spiritual assignments (whether new or existing) must be seen in light of a sovereign God. The blessing to be able to serve the Lord in their current capacities must be stated repeatedly.

God has privileged them to serve in their unique and meaningful capacity. Mentors must find new and creative ways to help Q4 members utilize their genuine faith and in some cases their life experiences to reach other people. They want to have an impact, and mentors must help them find the right opportunities. They want to be loved as equal partners for the cause of Christ and not forgotten. Pray.

In conclusion, the purpose of this chapter is to make Christians think and examine themselves. I must confess it has made me realize just how little faith I have. It would be nice if I could unequivocally say that I am a Q3 Christian, but with a good conscience, I cannot. As I read through the attributes of a Q3 Christian written above, I realized how far away I am from this perfect ideal of Christianity. I simply need to do a much better job of living by faith and trusting Him for every aspect of my life. God wants me to trust Him with my past, fears, ambition, and the totality of my life.

What about you? What aspect of this chapter has given you pause to re-evaluate and hit the restart button of your Christian faith? Are you willing to get to the next level of your spiritual growth? No one ever said that the Christian race would be void of frustration and defeat. However, the Bible does tell us that we can rest in Him and experience the true joy of being born-again. Are you a Q3 or a Q4 Christian? Are you actively striving toward the goal of having great faith and good works in your spiritual walk with Him?

3

KEEPING THE MAJESTY OF IT ALL

Christians need an awe-inspired state of mind and
worship that lead us to the most elevated comprehension
of His might and wonder.

FOLLOWERS OF JESUS CHRIST yearn to keep their faith filled with the love, joy, excitement, and hope necessary to live out a majestic and glorious manifestation of their Christian faith. Who would ever disagree with that premise? Each of us wants to reside and take refuge in the shadow of His wings while experiencing the most exhilarating and personal relationship with God as possible. While pressures and circumstances may temporarily get us down, we pray that God would once again elevate us to that still, small place of everlasting hope. That innate yearning to be with the Lord and please Him is hardwired into our Christian DNA when we accept Christ as our Savior. We forever desire to be with Him in eternity.

> For we know that if our earthly house of [this] taber-
> nacle were dissolved, we have a building of God, an
> house not made with hands, eternal in the heavens.
> For in this we groan, earnestly desiring to be clothed
> upon with our house which is from heaven: If so be
> that being clothed we shall not be found naked. (2
> Cor. 5:1–3)

Many of us start out like gangbusters with a singular focus on Jesus Christ and His Word, only to be sidetracked with the cares and entanglements of this present world. Unfortunately, some of those cares and entanglements may even involve brothers and sisters in Christ who are part of His church. These issues of life stand at the periphery of human importance and doctrinal significance but trap us in the quicksand of Christian mediocracy.

> For if after they have escaped the pollutions of the world through the knowledge of the Lord and Saviour Jesus Christ, they are again entangled therein, and overcome, the latter end is worse with them than the beginning. (2 Pet. 2:20)

If we agree that the pollutions of the world entangle us, what is the solution? If we know that our old man in the flesh is still lurking around, how do we overcome the crushing weight of temptation? Christians know the answer. We yield and trust in Him; we set no wicked thing before our eyes; we live disciplined Christian lives; we put on the mind of Christ; we learn to exude an agape type of love directed to God and our neighbors while walking and living in the Spirit of God.

There are so many Bible verses that are direct and to the point that help instruct us along the way. However, I believe that Jesus Christ has given us an additional answer in one of the most unlikely places possible. This answer is hidden in a place that may not be so obvious. He did so through a simple question when being arrested by the chief priests, Pharisees, officers, and a band of men:

> Jesus therefore, knowing all things that should come upon him, went forth, and said unto them, *Whom seek ye*? (John 18:4)

While the question Christ asked wasn't directly and specifically addressing one's ability to see, live, and keep the majesty of it all, it did establish the ultimate foundation of our Christian faith. The descending wisdom that we glean from these verses more than answers our questions and points to the one true solution. First, we need to understand the intent of the question. Why would Jesus Christ, the God of the universe, ask such an obvious question? Was He asking a rhetorical question? Was Jesus simply trying to ascertain what they wanted? No, probably not. The omniscient God of this universe already knew the answer.

Christ knew that the time had come to fulfill the most important and sacred sacrifice of all time, His timely and planned death. He knew that the Father asked him to selflessly lay down His life and be the propitiation for our sins, and thus perfect every blood sacrifice for God since the beginning of time. He also knew that His shed blood would be the only vehicle possible to reconcile sinful men to a holy and righteous God. Much like an attorney, I believe that God was establishing a record by asking the question.

Oftentimes an attorney will submit specific pieces of evidence in a trial and "for the record" that establishes vital information in support of their client's position. When arguing on their client's behalf, they simply want to signify and highlight specific facts that are foundational to the case and documented for future reference. I believe this is exactly what Jesus Christ was doing when he asked, "*Whom seek ye?*" He wanted to establish "for the record" and posterity the answer to His question:

> They answered him, *Jesus of Nazareth.* Jesus saith unto them, I am *he.* And Judas also, which betrayed him, stood with them. As soon then as he had said unto them, I am *he,* they went backward, and fell to the ground. Then asked he them again, *Whom seek ye?* And they said, *Jesus of Nazareth.* Jesus answered, I

have told you that I am *he*: if therefore ye seek me, let
these go their way: (John 18:5–8)

The answer given to the most important question ever asked
throughout eternity was placed in the annals of time and forever
documented "for the record." The answer was Jesus of Nazareth.
Not only did Jesus want to get it on the record, much like an attorney, But He also repeated and confirmed the answer a second
time.

These men were not seeking a religious sect or group of anti-
establishment cult members. They were seeking the Son of the living God. Christ was telling all of eternity that these men were
there seeking to destroy the Savior, not a group of dissidents. For
it was not a radical group of dissidents who hung on the cross and
shed their blood for the sins of mankind—it was Jesus Christ!
Only He could be the substitute for our sins and reconcile us to
God.

The record had to show they were seeking Jesus. This fact is
foundational to our faith. While we (Christians) positionally identify with the death, burial, and resurrection of Jesus Christ, only
He could have hung on the Cross of Calvary. Let the prophetic
record show that it was Jesus of Nazareth. Let us now return to
the solution we seek.

As Christians, we are able to keep the majesty of it all with a
singular focus on Jesus Christ. We should be awestruck, inspired,
and in a reverent state of worship with the corresponding understanding of our infinitesimal stature of nothingness. When we get
our arms around who He is as God Almighty compared to who
we are in the flesh, the floodgates of wisdom and blessing will
overwhelm us. One can only wonder in amazement that He cares
for us and considers us at all since we are such despicable and
sinful creatures in our Adamic sin natures. When we do keep a
singular focus, we are reestablishing the vital precedent and rec-

ord-containing fact submitted so long ago (in the court of injustice) ... the wonderful and marvelous answer ... Jesus of Nazareth.

> For of him, and through him, and to him, are all
> things: to whom be glory for ever. Amen.
> (Rom. 11:36)

Within the last year, I had a wonderful conversation with a former Pastor, who said something that stuck with me. He stated, "It's all about Jesus, and the rest is a bunch of fluff." When you boil it all down, he, too, understands the significance of keeping our eyes on Jesus and Him alone. When we do, the majesty of it all will come clearly into focus and the clutter of the world will quickly dissipate.

In the words of Lela B. Long, "Jesus, Jesus, Jesus, sweetest name I know. Fills my every longing. Keeps me singing as I go."

4

THE SPIRITUAL REALMS OF AFFLICTION

The severity and uniqueness of our trials are purposefully designed toward our bent.

THE GOD OF THIS universe has created our existence here on earth with a number of pressure points that help refine our spiritual progress toward a sanctified state of being. He has our best interests at heart and wants to get us battle-tested and battle-ready prior to entering the gates of heaven. Complain, spit, and sputter, as we will, but the fact remains that He desires to change us for His glory.

God is going to use every means available to Him to help us achieve the desired ends. The severity and uniqueness of one's trials are perfectly designed for the conditions of one's personhood. Only He knows the entirety of our inner bent and idiosyncratic nature. Only He completely understands us.

While God will never directly use the forces of evil himself, He has allowed the existence of evil to pervade; the trials of our mind to help us become more discerning Christians; and the trials of our culture, family life, and the necessary godly trials of affliction to help shape us. Those are five separate and distinct realms of affliction that we are going to review in this chapter. While God is sovereign over each, the cause-and-effect relationships and motives within each realm have different outcomes.

The Lord will allow us to experience the refining fire of our spiritual awakening and/or rebirth for His eternal glory.

> My son, despise not the chastening of the LORD; neither be weary of his correction: (Prov. 3:11)

Afflictions of the Mind

First, we have the affliction of the mind. One may even want to call this realm the self-affliction of the mind. For the sake of full visibility, this is without a doubt the most challenging area for me. It is the reason I listed it first. And, if I am guessing right, it is also one of the most challenging areas for most men. The old man in the flesh uses my mind as a torture chamber. Satan wants me to stay off-balance. He wants me to plant my feet in the mud and muck of the past, keeping me from advancing to the constancy of righteous thought.

Oftentimes, the mud and muck of the past spills over into the quicksand of the present, impacting the purity of my thought life. It is both frustrating and debilitating all at the same time. Discouragement, despondency, and the misery of dwelling in a place that is consumed with sin and iniquity is all around me and, at times, more than I can bear. In a real sense, I get to peek into a world that I no longer want to be in. These verses in Romans have never rung more true for me:

> For that which I do I allow not: for what I would, that do I not; but what I hate, that do I. If then I do that which I would not, I consent unto the law that it is good. Now then it is no more I that do it, but sin that dwelleth in me. For I know that in me (that is, in my flesh,) dwelleth no good thing: for to will is present with me; but how to perform that which is good I find not. For the good that I would I do not: but the evil which I would not, that I do. Now if I do that I would

not, it is no more I that do it, but sin that dwelleth in me. I find then a law, that, when I would do good, evil is present with me. For I delight in the law of God after the inward man: But I see another law in my members, warring against the law of my mind, and bringing me into captivity to the law of sin which is in my members. O wretched man that I am! who shall deliver me from the body of this death? (Rom. 7:15–24)

Maybe you, too, experience affliction of the mind with undisciplined and untamed thoughts. If so, perhaps your prayer will go something like this:

Dear Lord, help me condition my mind with Bible truths and the things of God where my mind becomes blind to any glimpse of unholy and unrighteous thinking. Don't allow me to set any wicked thing before my eyes or my mind! Allow me to commit the entirety of my works to you so that you can establish my thinking. Help me to only consider, dwell on, and engage in thoughts that are virtuous in nature. Please, Lord, draw me closer to you by the righteous thinking of my mind. Help me to flee youthful lusts and wrong-minded thinking. Help me not be my own worst enemy. Help me to claim Philippians 4:8 as the spiritual balm needed to ensure the purity of my thought life.

Finally, brethren, whatsoever things are true, whatsoever things are honest, whatsoever things are just, whatsoever things are pure, whatsoever things are lovely, whatsoever things are of good report; if there be any virtue, and if there be any praise, think on these things. (Phil. 4:8)

God's Trials of Affliction

Next, we have the afflictions generated from the prodding, chastening, and reproving of a loving God. He often goes to extraordinary lengths to put us in positions of spiritual discomfort, sharpening our heavenly resolve. We live in the experiences and context that He has created for us, helping us to reconcile and understand the significance of each teaching moment. Just think about the spiritual challenges we face when we are asked to be in the world, but not of the world. We are to venture out by faith into the world and redeem the times but still walk that blessed tightrope of separation by not letting it condition or diminish our testimonies for the Lord. One would say that it is a perfect testing and proving ground.

When we add in all the potential impediments to walking in the Spirit, which include the pressures of our stewardship responsibilities to money, relationships, speech, vocations, and to the church, then the totality of God's refining hand seems insurmountably real. Yet He tells us to run the race with patience. I don't know about you, but that specific encouragement from God seems to be paradoxical. I have run a few races in my day and patience is not something that comes immediately to mind. However, God is telling us in His Word to have patience, peace, and humility while diligently running the obstacle course of life. When we throw off the shackles of the old man and put on the mind of Christ, we can finish the course and win the race of the Christian life with honor.

Fortunately, the race God has chosen is clearly defined with identifying markers that tell us what both in bounds and out of bounds entail. Through the guidance of His Word and the elevated spiritual state of our conscience (Holy Spirit), we can maneuver with the discernment necessary to finish the course. God tells us to keep our eyes straight ahead as we run, turning neither to the left nor to the right. In the race determined, He has provided that sacred beacon of light (Jesus Christ) to us as the only true focal point of illumination. He is our locus of control! We are to be diligent, skillful, and lawful in our race as we press toward the mark and the rewards set before us. When we step out of bounds in the Christian race God has called us to, the weight and pressure of our sin will make us come to a screeching halt or, at the very least, to a slow and ineffectual crawl.

> Wherefore seeing we also are compassed about with so great a cloud of witnesses, let us lay aside every weight, and the sin which doth so easily beset us, and let us run with patience the race that is set before us, Looking unto Jesus the author and finisher of our faith; who for the joy that was set before him endured the cross, despising the shame, and is set down at the right hand of the throne of God. (Heb. 12:1–2)

At the same time, God has provided a race track that is wide enough in which to maneuver. With our unique characteristics, spiritual gifts, and personality traits, we are given the freedoms necessary to choose. God is telling us that He has given us a wide road in which to operate (free will) within specified and defined barriers of construction (His sovereignty). God is saying, "Here is the road that you can use for your Christian race, now honor and glorify me by choosing wisely." He loves us and will never leave or forsake us (Heb. 13:5). He will be with us even unto the end of the world (Matt. 28:20). We must remember that each trial that God puts in our way is for our own good.

> And we know that all things work together for good to them that love God, to them who are the called according to his purpose. (Rom. 8:28)

Satan's Trials of Affliction

The next trial that we face is from our adversary, the devil. Sometimes it feels like we face unrelenting and ongoing temptations in the flesh that have been orchestrated by the prince of this world. Satan's original work in the Garden of Eden has left mankind with an Adamic and fallen sin nature. It is a blemish that can only be reconciled through the precious blood of Jesus Christ our Lord. All Christians must wrestle with the old man within. God wants the best for His children and uses a loving and guiding hand while Satan has a contrary motive and is in the business of conquest. He does so with a subtle and deceitful claw.

> Be sober, be vigilant; because your adversary the devil, as a roaring lion, walketh about, seeking whom he may devour: (1 Pet. 5:8)

A fallen Lucifer hopes to reestablish his authority and reign of terror. Satan wants to rule and reign in God's place, establishing his own kingdom. His kingdom would be an inauthentic copy of a superior being's (The Great I AM) holy and righteous creation.

> How art thou fallen from heaven, O Lucifer, son of the morning! how art thou cut down to the ground, which didst weaken the nations! For thou hast said in thine heart, I will ascend into heaven, I will exalt my throne above the stars of God: I will sit also upon the mount of the congregation, in the sides of the north: I will ascend above the heights of the clouds; I will be like the most High. (Isa. 14:12–14)

Cultural Trials of Affliction

Beyond the three trials of affliction discussed above, what is most fascinating to me is how God allows those trials of affliction to be played out in a cultural dynamic. The stage He created provides numerous cultural manifestations and spiritual domains. The family, ministry, arts and entertainment, sport, educational, vocational, and political realms help support and/or influence the determination of each of these trials.

Based on the vitriol and hatred toward Christians in our current culture, I would argue that the culture itself is definitely a fourth trial of affliction. Humanity stands at the gates of spiritual freedom readying the cultural ax of temptation and destruction. The world in which we live is ready to consume their own unless a predetermined script of anti-God beliefs are adhered to hook, line, and sinker. Christians will be persecuted and attacked for anything less than humanity's ideal.

Familial Trials of Affliction

While our family members are not out to hurt us or to ruin us, the relationships that we encounter in the family structure are additional trials that help us grow. Husband/wife, sister/brother, parent/child, and the relationships between friends are challenging. These relationships can drive us to our knees, begging God to give us both patience and understanding. At other times, we respond in the flesh, exacerbating contentious and out-of-control sentiments and responses. For the most part, our homes and family members are a safe haven from spiritual unrest. However, as we have all experienced, that it is not the case in every instance. We fail, learn, and grow.

In conclusion, I hope that this chapter has heightened your awareness of the trials of affliction that we must overcome for the glory of God. We must understand that God has designed it that way for our spiritual benefit. The trials are a complex web of en-tanglements, frustrations, relationships, mountaintops, escape hatches, and pleasures of joy in the race HE has commissioned specifically for you. He loves us. As a Father who intensely loves His children, He wants the best for us spiritually:

> For whom the Lord loveth he chasteneth, and scour-geth every son whom he receiveth. (Heb. 12:6)

How is your race going? Do you have the sacred beacon of light (Jesus Christ) guiding you toward heaven? Are you able to see the clearly defined markers along the way? Are you using the choices, freedoms, and liberties He has given us for God's glory and not making an occasion for the flesh?

5

BLESSING IN INDIA

Faith becomes increasingly manifest in our daily walk as
we travel through the long and arduous tunnel of life
seeing periods of both extreme darkness and vibrancy of
light, never losing sight of the one true focal point ... the
lighthouse of Jesus Christ our Lord.

WHERE DO I BEGIN? How do I put into words the blessings and memories of India in any meaningful way that will convey its lasting spiritual significance on the attendees? God allowed me the opportunity to teach and preach in the country of India. There were so many precious moments and teaching opportunities that will be cherished for a lifetime. While the motivation for attending the conference in India was to teach and preach about leadership in a workplace environment for the benefit of others, the lessons of leadership came back in my direction many times over because of the sweet spirit of the Christians there. I was the one being taught and convicted about true servant leadership. In the First Annual Good News 360 Leadership Conference, we had a tremendous diversity of believers heralding from many walks of life. There were those who came from villages, full-time ministry, tent-making ministry, farmers, university students, engineers, government officials, nonprofits, and others who are committed to living a nomadic existence going from village to village proclaiming the sacred gospel message of Christ and living by faith. Their individual stories and callings are all special and unique. It was demonstrably apparent that the tie that binds their Christian love is Jesus Christ our Lord and Savior. They make it evident in practicing true servant leadership in everything they do and say.

Their humility and deference to others and to those in authority hits one like a ton of bricks. They espouse others before themselves, living the embodiment of sacrifice and selfless love that puts the needs of others before their own. The Christians in India exude a natural self-expression (God-given) of humility and servant leadership that overpowers you when you are around them. It is part of their makeup and who they are as humble Christian believers serving a risen Savior.

The extension of love, concern, and heartfelt appreciation for others permeated every aspect of the conference. The conference had as its central focus the theme of servant leadership. I am pleased to say that everyone I met from the group of 800 participants strongly exhibited this godly characteristic, including the leadership team and regional coordinators. Our comfort and well-being were foremost on their mind. I can't express enough thanks and gratitude for their watch care over us during our stay.

And while our hosts were exemplary in the way they practiced servant leadership by serving us and each other, we also got a real glimpse of the desperate spiritual needs of the country of India, which has a population of more than a billion people. The need is overwhelming. India is made up of approximately 79% Hindu, 15% Muslim, and 2.7% Christians, with the remaining religious factions making up the difference.

The country is filled with the hustle and bustle of everyday life and living, with people constantly on the go and in perpetual motion. While in the beautiful city of Hyderabad, we got to see some amazing things. We stopped in a predominantly Muslim neighborhood and got within close proximity of a local mosque and watched as they had their "call to prayer." We visited a local shopping area where vendors were peddling their wares and security was tight.

We also experienced what I will call "extreme" cab riding, which is nothing out of the ordinary for the citizens of the country. There was a 10-minute shouting match (gentlemanly discussion) between the cab driver and another vehicle after a small collision (very typical). After some lengthy haggling, the cabby deposited a small sum of money into the hand of the "victim" that was proportional to the offense, and we were once again on our way. It was one of several incidents we experienced while on the roads in Hyderabad. If you ever have the pleasure of hailing a cab in one of the metropolitan cities of India, you are in for a real treat! The experience is something you will not soon forget.

My final impression of India was reserved especially for me. It occurred when boarding a plane traveling from Hyderabad to Mumbai on my way home (traveling alone). God had a teaching moment for me. While waiting to board the plane, I tried to catch a little nap. The first time I awoke, I noticed a large-framed man in his 30s staring at me from a few rows across the way. He didn't seem particularly happy to see me. His big, dark eyes were quite ominous looking. In fact, the first time we locked eyes, I felt like I was looking at something very evil. I decided to bounce my eyes and focus on something else and promptly fell back to sleep.

When I woke up again, the same thing happened. This man seemed like he was trying to stare a hole right through me. I decided right then that I wouldn't look his way again so as not to provoke him. About 15 minutes later, we started to board the plane. I sat down at my window seat about three quarters of the way down on the left side of the large jumbo jet as it slowly filled up. Guess who sat down right next to me? Yup, it was the gentlemen in the airport who couldn't keep his eyes off of me. I must confess, I wasn't too excited about this "chance" encounter.

My instincts were right on target. This radicalized Muslim proceeded to take out his computer device and blast anti-American propaganda and death to the infidels as loud as the computer would allow. He then proceeded to another site on his computer where they talked about the blessings of 9/11 and of the slaughter of innocent civilians. Well, it was a moment of truth and one that I will not soon forget.

I decided not to antagonize the man. I simply turned my head to the window, closed my eyes, and prayed. Very shortly thereafter, a couple of other Indian men approached and told my "new friend" that he was in their seat. The radicalized Muslim then got up and moved to his assigned seat. Yes, you got it! The Muslim purposefully sought me out for intimidation purposes. He sought me out to tell me that he didn't want me in his country again. Satan was telling me never to come back to the country of India. All these thoughts and more were swirling through my head as my "new friend" went back to his seat.

After all the joy and blessing of the leadership conference, was this going to be my lasting impression of India? Lord, why did you send a radicalized Muslim to try to intimidate me 8,000 miles away from home while traveling alone? What are you trying to show and teach me?

As I sat there contemplating what had just happened, thoughts about resting and trusting in my Savior started pouring forth, with numerous verses coming to mind. However, the story was not quite over. Once my "new friend" departed and the rightful owner of the seat sat down, I began to focus on the blessings of God and the spiritual significance of the situation. It just so happened that the second Indian who sat next to me was a born-again believer in Christ Jesus! What an opportunity we had over the next half hour to share with one another about God's providence, protection, and divine intervention.

We are in a spiritual warfare in high places. There are spiritual forces of evil, destruction, and death on the one hand. On the other, there are spiritual forces of goodness, love, and light. God was telling me that I will undoubtedly encounter evil forces from time to time in my short ambassadorship here on earth. He was also reminding me that He is sufficient. In the end, God wins the victory. He binds Satan for 1,000 years and subsequently casts him into the lake of fire. The enemy has no chance when going up against God, encroaching His power and fighting the eternal and everlasting power of the Holy Spirit.

God was also reminding me through this situation that the forces of good will always prevail. I am simply to take refuge in the shadow of His wings and call upon Him in times of trouble. Praise God for the wonderful and successful trip to India. I wouldn't have changed a thing. The people of India are a blessing, and I hope to return soon! My lasting impression of India is a great one! It is a country where Christians abound with servant leaders' hearts and where the need to proclaim Christ to unbelievers is everywhere!

6

CLOSING THE LEADERSHIP GAP

The romanticism of "the going" stirs the embers of our human emotions; while the reality of the service awakens us to the average and ordinary blessings of life hidden in the recesses of daily living.

THE LORD ALLOWED ME to share an illustration in a speaking opportunity that greatly resonated with an audience at a local public university. This audience was primarily a non-Christian group (approximately 120) who were searching for the meaning of life and leadership. These participants consisted of professors and other academics of higher education and learning along with some business professionals thrown into the mix. They were genuine and authentic individuals who were desperately trying to understand the dynamics of leadership and how they could impact the world.

I sincerely enjoyed getting to know many of them as individuals. I felt privileged in that moment to be used of the Lord for His honor and glory. I didn't share any revolutionary insights, nor did I touch on some magnificent new leadership model that would inspire people around the globe. To the contrary, I related my experiences and my journey as a professional baseball player (minor leagues) as an analogy to the mastery of leadership. This simple illustration opened the door for me to share the gospel message of Jesus Christ our Lord with many of the participants! Praise the Lord!

There are millions of baseball fans around the world who really enjoy the game. Many are season ticket holders who passionately attend as many games as they possibly can. You even hear of some older folks who are getting way up there in age who have not missed a game in literally decades. I guess you could say that they are rabid fans! Hats off to them and their dedication to their respective teams and the game of baseball.

These fans sit in the stands and watch, cheer, and learn many of the intricacies of the game. Many of them become so involved that they know the player's nicknames, idiosyncratic habits while standing at the plate, deficiencies and tendencies of the players while batting and hitting the ball, along with an in-depth understanding of the rules of the game.

It is quite fun and pleasurable to be around these baseball fans! I could sit for hours conversing with these individuals because they are so full of knowledge and facts. Sometimes they even get a little "crazy" when cheering on their teams or favorite players. Some of you can relate and probably understand what I mean.

What also fascinates me is the diversity of people sitting in the stands, with little-to-no commonality with one another on the major issues of life. In the normal course of the day, chances are that they would never bump into one another. They are simply baseball fanatics cheering for the team. These fans consist of various nationalities, levels of education and income, along with major differences in their values, standards, and personal beliefs.

Yes, by sitting in the stands, this diverse group of people have a good grasp of the game. But for many, that is where their understanding of baseball stops. Their knowledge reaches a plateau and then comes to an abrupt halt. Sitting in the stands and observing the game confines the participants to a contextual understanding of the game of baseball that, by necessity, puts a ceiling on their ability to exhibit a mastery of the game.

You can't master the game of baseball from the stands. Participation in the game is a prerequisite to a complete and holistic understanding of what it means to play baseball. You must be "in the game" to truly comprehend the beauty of the game. Don't get me wrong, the fans sitting in the box seats or bleachers are an absolute blast! They're fun to be around, as we have a common passion for a sport. However, trust me when I say that it is a form of understanding, and not the depth, breadth, and comprehension of understanding needed that comes as a natural (God-given) self-expression of the game. For example, I encourage you to try to deal with a 100-mile-per-hour fastball from the stands as a "bleacher creature!" Well, you get the point.

As a professional athlete, there are so many ingredients that go into and contribute to the mastery of the game of baseball. First, there is the preparation. Elite baseball players spend thousands of hours off the field honing their craft. Whether it is the batting cage, weight room, film room, agility training, or taking ground balls or fly balls from a coach, preparation is vital for the mastery of baseball. However, even with all the preparation, you still are not a complete player.

Second, it is the game conditions themselves that will bring you to a level of competence, knowledge, understanding, and proficiency that will allow you to master the game. It is learning to adjust to those 100 mile-per-hour fastballs mentioned above, slow curve balls, sliders, or knuckle balls in game conditions that get you to the next level of mastery. It is learning to run down long fly balls or gauging the distance to the fence that can only be realized during high-pressure game conditions.

Third, the language of baseball in game conditions is part of that holistic and comprehensive understanding that leads to mastery. There is a conversational domain in the game of baseball that is unique and specific to those at the highest levels. They speak an entirely different language—the language of baseball mastery. That language of communication takes many different forms. Body language, sign language, terms, and phraseology all contribute to a unique conversational domain that distinguishes those sitting in the stands from those who have decided to put themselves "in the game" of baseball.

There also comes a point when you are at the top of your game (mastery) when everything starts to slow down. Athletes call it "being in the zone." For baseball players, it is when they walk up to the plate and there is complete silence. That silence comes from an indescribable and intense focus. As a player, you hear nothing and see nothing except the pitcher. Everything seems to be happening in slow motion, and the baseball looks like a big, fat watermelon coming to the plate. I almost hate to say it, but hitting the ball seems way too easy in those particular moments.

As a result of the preparation, work, dedication, and swings at the bat in game conditions, you have now entered the mastery phase of the game. The "zone" does not happen often for professional athletes; however, when it does, it can't be missed. In baseball terminology, you are on fire!

Fourth, the level of commitment to rise to the level of an elite athlete and to be viewed as a "master" of the game comes at great personal sacrifice and cost. In a sense, baseball becomes a part of who you are as a person. Professional athletes drink, sleep, and eat baseball. They hang out with other baseball players, eat meals together, work out at the gym together and, for the most part, are part of similar social circles.

As I began relating this story to many of the university participants while witnessing to them about their need for a Savior, I tried to delicately and diplomatically relate the analogy back to Christianity. The church is full of people sitting in the stands with an abundance of knowledge about the Christian faith. These individuals understand the language of Christianity, church customs, how to deliver awesome prayers, and may even spend countless hours studying the Word of God. You would be impressed with their knowledge.

It would seem as though these individuals get Christianity. However, they have never been able to master the natural (God-given) self-expression of the Christian faith because they are satisfied with viewing their faith from the stands of life. A comfortable place to be sure! They may even be born-again believers who made a decision to accept Christ as their Savior.

The problem with this approach and perspective is a real lack of depth in real-world or game experience. They are sitting in the stands right next to the "mixed multitude." Their ability to make adjustments to the 100-mile-an-hour fastballs is lacking. Their growth opportunities as believers are lacking compared to those who put themselves right dab in the middle of the Christian walk. Yes, I am talking about much more than talking a good game. I am expressing our responsibility to pull up our boot straps and genuinely and authentically be committed to the works of the faith of Jesus Christ.

> Be ye doers of the word, and not hearers only, deceiving your own selves. (Jas. 1:22)

While the works of our labor will in no way add to our salvation experience, once saved, we are expected to exercise our spiritual gifts in a leadership capacity. We are expected to be "in the game" of our Christian faith.

In summary, we desperately need to focus on "closing the leadership gap" between the stands and game conditions of our Christian faith. For many of us, the divide between these two positions has put us in a place where we are not fully usable for our Lord. The potential to impact the world with the gospel message becomes limited as we learn about Christianity, cheer on those involved in the game, but remain content to sit in the stands. Our ability to demonstrate a *Christian leadership worldview* will be greatly thwarted and minimized. God has given us the power through the Holy Spirit to step up and lead. Will you step up to the plate and start taking swings at the ball in game conditions? Are you committed to a holistic comprehension of the mastery of your Christian faith? Which script on your tombstone will be most appropriate?

> Here lies a wonderful, knowledgeable, compassionate, loving, Christian man or woman who lived their Christian life to the fullest with great exuberance, while sitting in the stands of their Christian faith.

OR

> Here lies a wonderful, knowledgeable, compassionate, loving, Christian man or woman who lived their Christian life to the fullest with great exuberance, who closed the leadership gap by getting in the game of their Christian faith and leading.

Won't you step out today and make a decision to be a leader and impact others? Please, get in the game!

> Also, I heard the voice of the Lord, saying, Whom shall I send, and who will go for us? Then said I, Here am I; send me. (Isa. 6:8)

> But ye shall receive power, after that the Holy Ghost is come upon you: and ye shall be witnesses unto me both in Jerusalem, and in all Judea, and in Samaria, and unto the uttermost part of the earth. (Acts 1:8)

> Let a man so account of us, as of the ministers of Christ, and stewards of the mysteries of God. (1 Cor. 4:1)

7

DOES AMERICA BLUSH ANYMORE?

We are set apart for holy and righteous means, never gravitating toward anything that would resemble an unholy alliance with sin and iniquity.

WHEN IS THE LAST time you were so embarrassed that you blushed at something that went against the core of who you are as a Christian? Seriously, can you point to an occasion(s) where you were so incredibly overwhelmed and convicted that you had to bow your head in shame and acknowledge the error of your ways and/or the ways of your countrymen? Can you quickly refer to a situation(s) that was so deeply profound that you knew it was going against the very nature and moral character of an Almighty God? In other words, the situation stopped you dead in your tracks and made you feel uneasy to the point of being "red-faced."

Let me help you! Perhaps there was an event, conversation, comment, television show, improper joke, thought, lifestyle, or song that was demonstratively anti-God and impacted you to the point of shamefacedness. There may have even been a conscious decision to use the liberty that we have in Christ as an occasion for the flesh that made you ashamed. Have you found yourself running swiftly down the road of iniquity and perdition only to get entangled in the quicksand of life?

Let me be blunt. America doesn't blush anymore because she is attached at the hip with our culture, period. This includes born-again believers who would consider themselves fundamental in their beliefs. We have become so desensitized to sin that it just doesn't bother us like it used to. The aggregate exposure to the sinful ways of this world has conditioned us to be comfortable with the culture. However, we sure can talk a good game on Sundays. We talk like we are living holy and righteous lives to perfection, all the while deeply entrenched in worldly lusts, habits, and thinking. God help us!

In the Old Testament, when Ezra and Jeremiah looked around, they also saw the blatant disregard for the holy and righteous nature of the Lord our God. All the training, teaching, counsel, encouragement, correction, and commands slowly dissipated to the point where the Israelites started to look just like the culture. At the time, it appeared that the Israelites were creating the wicked culture that God told them to avoid. They were involved in mixed marriages with heathens (Canaanites, Hittites, and others), idolatry, and other forms of pagan worship and ritualistic sin.

However, what is even more saddening is the role that the leaders of that day played in that development. Our Judeo-Christian forefathers decided to sit on the sidelines of life and do nothing, or, at the very least, they participated in creating the mess they were experiencing. Generation after generation had slowly drifted by where toleration, inclusivity, and the allure of sin took root, creating callouses so tough that any resemblance of holiness was now gone.

In two verses of the book of Jeremiah (written below), the Lord indicated that "neither could they blush." Ezra himself was so ashamed that he had trouble lifting his face:

> And said, O my God, I am ashamed and blush to lift up my face to thee, my God: for our iniquities are increased over our head, and our trespass is grown up unto the heavens. (Ezra 9:6)

Were they ashamed when they had committed abomination? nay, they were not at all ashamed, neither could they blush: therefore they shall fall among them that fall: at the time that I visit them they shall be cast down, saith the LORD. (Jer. 6:15)

Were they ashamed when they had committed abomination? nay, they were not at all ashamed, neither could they blush: therefore shall they fall among them that fall: in the time of their visitation they shall be cast down, saith the LORD. (Jer. 8:12)

What an indictment coming from the Creator of the world, God Almighty! He was telling them that they were so consumed with worldly pleasures and the sins of this world that He would cast them down. However, in order to fully understand the severity and depth of the indictment, we must first explore those natural and moral godly characteristics mentioned earlier in this chapter. It is only when we get an up-close and personal glimpse of who He actually is in comparison to our lowly human state that our hearts should be melted before Him.

God's Natural Characteristics

Omnipotent – He is an all-powerful God. No one can resist His authority and rule over the universe. He alone has the power to reign on-high! Because of His omnipotence, His will on this earth will ultimately be accomplished.

Omniscience – He is all-knowing. As the Alpha and Omega, He knows all things. He knows the thoughts and intents of the heart of mankind. His thoughts and wisdom are beyond human imagination.

Omnipresence – God is everywhere all at the same time. He is an active participant in the lives of Christians everywhere to the fullest extent of His being, endeavoring to mold them into His image.

Immutable – God never changes. He is the same since the beginning of time. This consistency of character gives faith and hope to believers. He does not lie, exaggerate, or change the essence of His character. We can truly rely on the great "I Am."

God's Moral Characteristics

Merciful – God withholds the things that we do deserve. In our natural sin state, we are guilty before the judge of this world. He mercifully stayed our execution when he sent His Son as our substitute on the Cross of Calvary.

Grace – God's unmerited favor. There is nothing that we can do or add to our salvation experience to gain favor with God. It is a free gift bestowed on us from above. This favor rests in His unfathomable love for His children.

Love – This love is so intense that He sent His Son to die for us. This love demanded that He turn His back and separate Himself from our Lord and Saviour Jesus Christ. Since God can't be in the presence of sin, total separation was required from His Son when Christ died and was in the belly of the earth. This was an agape love that will only be completely understood when we are with Him in heaven.

Truth – God is truth. Absolute truth begins and ends with His Word. God's Word was verbally inspired and is without error. Simply put, the Word of God is perfect, as He is perfect!

Justice – He is the judge of this world. God hates sin. The only sin that He will not pardon is the rejection of His Son. His standing as judge is without argument based on the essence of who He is. He created the laws that govern the universe and beyond, and as such, it is He who stands supreme as the ultimate judge.

Righteousness – God will always do what is right. His divine nature doesn't allow Him to be less than perfect in all His ways. Since God does not make any mistakes, His righteousness will always prevail.

Holiness – God hates sin because His character is consumed with holiness – a state of being that demands excommunication from the evils of this world. His holiness can be illustrated and supported by many of the words in the following verse:

> Finally, brethren, whatsoever things are true, whatsoever things are honest, whatsoever things are just, whatsoever things are pure, whatsoever things are lovely, whatsoever things are of good report; if there be any virtue, and if there be any praise, think on these things. (Phil. 4:8)

Yes, America needs to get to the point where she blushes again. She should blush because people like Ezra and Jeremiah and others are willing to step out and cry against the ills of this present culture. She should blush because we have Christian leaders who are empowered by the Spirit of the Living God to take up the cause and fight. However, she should blush primarily because she comes under the conviction and shame of her sin by the impact and awakening that the Word of God stirs in her heart. She should then fall prostrate before Him in the shadow of His wings for restoration and glory!

Oh, that America would start blushing again!

8

LEADERSHIP DEFINED

"Bust down the doors and take no prisoners," cries the self-proclaimed leader of men; while the Christian leader unassumingly asks, "How can I serve to the glory of God?"

SINCE THE RELEASE OF my first book titled, *The Christian Leader's Worldview*, I have been fielding questions on how I landed on the definition of leadership that was included at the beginning of the book. Just prior to the table of contents there is a declaration of what I believe to be an appropriate definition of leadership. It was a sincere and honest attempt to capture the most critical elements of leadership, while documenting some of the mysteries found in the Word of God that are too difficult to reconcile this side of heaven. The following is a reprint of the definition found in the book:

> The thoughts, desires, passions, and actions of Christian men and women by the leading of the Holy Spirit and under God's control, for *selfless ends*.

When constructing this definition, I wanted to skillfully craft and design a definition that had impact and meaning to Christian leaders around the globe. I pray that the following commentary will provide additional valuable insight for a more comprehensive understanding of my definition of leadership, while challenging individuals to be more involved in the execution of the term.

Trinity

When contemplating this phenomenon called leadership in its absolute form, a definition would not be complete without first acknowledging the power of the Father, the Son, and the Holy Spirit. Yes, it is in the study of the divine personages and Godhead of the Trinity—with each of their unique and dynamic characteristics—that we begin to formulate the true starting point for a leadership definition. While we directly use the words "Holy Spirit" and "God" in our definition, the phrase "for selfless ends" is an indirect reference to our Lord and Savior Jesus Christ. Christ was the epitome of selflessness! We serve one God, in the form of three separate and distinct personalities that define who we are as leaders. Amen!

> Go ye therefore, and teach all nations, baptizing them in the name of the Father, and of the Son, and of the Holy Ghost: Teaching them to observe all things whatsoever I have commanded you: and, lo, I am with you always, even unto the end of the world. Amen. (Matt. 28:19–20)

Good Friends

Charles Spurgeon once commented when asked to choose between God's sovereignty (predestination) and human responsibility (man's free will) with a most succinct retort that had stinging and insightful impact. Spurgeon responded with the candor, grace, and depth that only he had the ability to articulate on this subject. He indicated (and I am paraphrasing) that he had no interest in choosing between two good friends. In our leadership definition, we simply wanted to acknowledge these two "good friends." We do not feel compelled to be divisive in any shape, form, or fashion on this issue. We have no desire to point out specific (or pet) passages that will dogmatically defend either of these positions in isolation.

We simply look to the totality of Scripture and respond with a resounding YES! Yes, we serve a God who is the Alpha and Omega that knows our charted course and paths in life along with our final appointment! Yes, we have the free will to make choices and decisions in life that will either glorify a Risen Savior or glorify self. On this topic, I am not able to conjure up any additional insight except it come from a place of human reasoning with little-to-no value. I simply look forward to entering heaven's gates to be able to understand the richness of these seemingly paradoxical doctrinal truths.

> He hath made the earth by his power, he hath established the world by his wisdom, and hath stretched out the heaven by his understanding. (Jer. 51:15)

> I call heaven and earth to record this day against you, that I have set before you life and death, blessing and cursing: therefore choose life, that thou and thy seed may live: (Deut. 30:19)

Servant Leadership

What a powerful leadership characteristic! Just think about it! The ability for leaders to be able to focus on someone beyond themselves is paramount to effective leadership. A servant leadership approach is vital to any real understanding of the term. Remember, we are not talking about coercion, brute force, dictatorship, brain washing, or tactics that manipulate an outcome. We are talking about the genuine and authentic desire to serve other people and their development in order to contribute to a broader purpose. When you enter that selfless realm of people building and have a genuine concern and love (agape love) for others, you enter the world of trust, hope, and confidence. Christ loved us with a love so strong (agape love) that he was willing to die that we might gain eternal life! The Apostle Paul also reminds us of our leadership responsibility relating to love (charity):

> And now abide faith, hope, charity, these three; but the greatest of these is charity. (1 Cor. 13:13)

> And he sat down, and called the 12, and saith unto them, If any man desire to be first, the same shall be last of all, and servant of all. (Mark 9:35)

Male and Female

Everyone who has accepted Christ as their Savior has been adopted into the family of God. A blessing and byproduct of that adoption is the empowering nature of the Holy Spirit along with the endowment of our God-given spiritual gifts. We are compelled to use those spiritual gifts for the edification of the church body! By definition and of necessity, those spiritual gifts demand leadership. We are required to exercise those gifts for the furtherance of His kingdom. Anything less will compromise the effective nature and working of the body of Christ. In our definition, we purposefully use the words "men" and "women" based on the particulars above. May all of our lights so shine before mankind as a lighthouse to the world!

> Let your light so shine before men, that they may see your good works, and glorify your Father which is in heaven. (Matt. 5:16)

Human Introspection

We will now mention the importance of self-examination on the nature of leadership. Leaders must continually be "on guard" and conscious of their thoughts, desires, passions, and actions. Leaders need to die to their "old man" daily and put on the mind of Christ. God has formed mankind with an indescribable web of complexity that allows us to think, feel, act, and make informed decisions. The left side of our brain thinks in ways that are logical and sequential while the right side of our brain is there for more creative and intuitive ways of thinking. It is only through deep self-examination, confession, and understanding that we reach a point where we can be used as leaders to impact others for Christ. We need to harness our thoughts, desires, passions, and actions through the filter of God's Word!

> Examine yourselves, whether ye be in the faith; prove your own selves. Know ye not your own selves, how that Jesus Christ is in you, except ye be reprobates? (2 Cor. 13:5)

Action / Execution

Here is where the rubber meets the road. Are you willing to step out by faith and do something? Are you willing to act? Will you challenge yourself to get involved and to be an active participant? What an awesome responsibility we have as leaders. We are called to be good Christian soldiers, preach and teach His Word, evangelize, and have dominion over the earth while involving ourselves in the lives of other people by building relationships! This means both action and discomfort. Leadership is hard. If you exercise true leadership, there will be peaks and valleys and times that you will question your own ability to lead. However, at these low points in your leadership development, God will move and teach you about the absolute and responsible nature of leadership.

> WHEREFORE seeing we also are compassed about with so great a cloud of witnesses, let us lay aside every weight, and the sin which doth so easily beset us, and let us run with patience the race that is set before us, Looking unto Jesus the author and finisher of our faith; who for the joy that was set before him endured the cross, despising the shame, and is set down at the right hand of the throne of God. (Heb. 12:1–2)

Results

Leaders are passionately committed to moving from point A to point B in whatever task or challenge is at hand. Yes, there is an end game. Leaders have a vision of the future that they try to communicate and make happen in order to achieve a result. However, as we have indicated above, those results should neither be self-aggrandizing, narcissistic, or focused on a desire to achieve personal and selfish gain. They are meant for "selfless ends" as indicated in our definition.

> I press toward the mark for the prize of the high calling of God in Christ Jesus. (Phil. 3:14)

In summary, leadership is a dynamic state of influence that starts with the shed blood of Jesus Christ. It is the recognition that God has equipped you for a cause much bigger than yourself. If you are willing to yield to the calling of leadership through your spiritual gifts, He will perform amazing things through you for His ultimate glory. I hope and pray that this additional discussion on our definition of leadership will inspire you to think more critically on the subject and form your own definition. Take the time right now and write down what leadership means to you! Is Christ both the starting and ending point for your definition?

9

CHRIST OUR GOVERNOR

Getting along requires self-denial, introspection, and the actions necessary for us to walk in the Spirit as we strive to impact the culture.

CHRISTIANS SHOULD TAKE GREAT comfort in knowing that Jesus Christ is the ruler of the universe. He alone is the mighty King who sits and reigns at the right hand of the Father. Everything that has been; everything that currently is; and everything that will be belongs to Him and Him alone. Fortunately for us, Christ has decided to designate human beings as the chosen vessels to help build His kingdom and to craft the perfect entrance for His second coming and eternal reign. Through our Spirit-led dominion, stewardship, and ambassadorial responsibilities, we help steer the course of humanity both in the physical and spiritual worlds.

It is God Who sets righteous kings on their thrones, and, yes, even allows evil despots to govern with outstretched arms of terror. Christ has absolute, unmitigated, and unquestioned authority. Christ is our sovereign sitting in the highest seat of government, and we serve at His pleasure. Yet, we grumble and complain and continue to question the supremacy of His authority. We often take our eyes off the ball, questioning the attributes, standards, and actions of the opposing political party currently in power and residing over the laws of our land. At times, we demonstrate a restlessness of soul and spirit with respect to the leaders He has placed over us.

Lord, please bring us back to a clear and full understanding of your sovereign power, which includes your governance here on earth. Help us to understand our role as Christians in the government of the United States of America along with its historical Christian roots and context. Let any man that will, who foolishly claims that America's historical record is not replete with evidence that the constituting of civil government in America was founded principally upon the Rock of Jesus Christ, take the time to read the excerpts below, and thereby become convinced of the errancy of his former historically unsustainable prejudice.[1] Help us to understand that there is "no king but King Jesus" and act accordingly!

> And I heard as it were the voice of a great multitude, and as the voice of many waters, and as the voice of mighty thunderings, saying, Alleluia: for the Lord God omnipotent reigneth. (Rev. 19:6)

> The king's heart is in the hand of the LORD, as the rivers of water: he turneth it whithersoever he will. (Prov. 21:1)

> For the kingdom is the LORD'S: and he is the governor among the nations. (Ps. 22:28)

> For unto us a child is born, unto us a son is given: and the government shall be upon his shoulder: and his name shall be called Wonderful, Counsellor, The mighty God, The everlasting Father, The Prince of Peace. (Isa. 9:6)

For the LORD is our judge, the LORD is our lawgiver, the LORD is our king; he will save us. (Isa. 33:22)

And Jesus came and spake unto them, saying, All power is given unto me in heaven and in earth. (Matt. 28:18)

In lieu of the verses (facts) above—which demonstrate that Jesus is our Sovereign Lord over all aspects of our government and the cultural manifestation of the body politic—how are Christian leaders, then, supposed to think about their role in a civil (governmental and public) capacity? I believe that Romans 1–7 sets the stage and begins to inform our minds as to our roles and responsibilities. God instructs us to respect and to be subject to the laws of the land. Government exists to be a minister of God for our good and to execute wrath on them that will do evil. We honor and give tribute to those who follow His biblical commands in this regard.

Let every soul be subject unto the higher powers. For there is no power but of God: the powers that be are ordained of God. Whosoever therefore resisteth the power, resisteth the ordinance of God: and they that resist shall receive to themselves damnation. For rulers are not a terror to good works, but to the evil. Wilt thou then not be afraid of the power? do that which is good, and thou shalt have praise of the same: For he is the minister of God to thee for good. But if thou do that which is evil, be afraid; for he beareth not the sword in vain: for he is the minister of God, a revenger to execute wrath upon him that doeth evil. Wherefore ye must needs be subject, not only for wrath, but also for conscience sake. For this cause pay ye tribute also: for they are God's ministers, attending continually upon this very thing. Render therefore to

all their dues: tribute to whom tribute is due; custom
to whom custom; fear to whom fear; honour to whom
honour. (Rom. 13:1–7)

Jesus tells us in His own words what the order of submission
and compliance should be relating to the laws of the land and to
the laws of an Almighty God:

And he said unto them, Render therefore unto Caesar
the things which be Caesar's, and unto God the things
which be God's. (Luke 20:25)

What happens, then, when an existing government becomes
misguided, enacting laws that contradict the supreme dictates
and principles of God? First, the U.S. court system must always
pursue the rigorous prosecution of all the laws of the land for
those who break them. Christians, too, must support the strict enforcement of the laws of the United States of America. It is only
by strict enforcement of our laws that civil society will flourish. In
general, I do believe that any legal system with a porous adherence to its laws will ultimately decline and disappear. However,
when there are unjust, antiquated, or misdirected laws in our
country (anti-God), then advocating for their removal and/or reconstitution must be pressed within the confines of civil obedience.

We must do everything within our power to get those laws
changed or overturned through the avenues available to us
within our constitution. It is our Christian duty. But we never
cede control of our liberty to live out our Christian existence, even
when in direct conflict with human governance. If our government stops being a minister of God for our good (good being defined by the principles in His Word) and in clear alignment with
His absolute authority in any manner whatsoever, then the Bible
gives us explicit instructions on *whom* to follow. We follow Christ.

I am reminded of a great American patriot and devout Christian named Samuel Adams. He was the cousin of our second President of the United States, John Adams. Samuel Adams had the perfect blend of character traits, including a revolutionary spirit; flare for the dramatics; an impetuous nature; and a Christian zeal that made him the right instrument (commissioned by God) to lead in many aspects of the birth of our great nation. His credentials and positions of leadership are well-documented and impressive—founding Father, delegate to the First Continental Congress, provincial congressman, state senator, delegate to the Second Continental Congress, lieutenant governor, and governor are some of the key platforms he used to serve our country.[2] As an ardent revolutionary, the rallying cry of him and his cronies (The Sons of Liberty) was, "There is no king but King Jesus." That is the spirit that must drive us forward. That is the spirit that should inform our politics and policies here in the government of the United States of America.

When we rest in the fact that the Lord is governor among the nations, it will change our disposition toward those with extreme or opposite views, allowing us to assume a more collegial tone— a tone, by the way, that is God-honoring, a tone to support one of the most glorious commandments of all—loving your neighbor as yourself. I pray that all Christians desire to serve their country, but most importantly that they desire to serve their God first. There is "no king but King Jesus!"

---

[1] http://www.daveblackonline.com/no_king_but_king_jesus.htm

[2] https://en.wikipedia.org/wiki/Samuel_Adams

10

MERRY CHRISTMAS

We have been given the secret keys to unlock the true
meaning of the fear of the Lord and find the knowledge of
God.

EACH CHRISTMAS SEASON, CHRISTIANS everywhere get invigor-
ated and overjoyed at the prospect of celebrating the birth of their
Savior, Jesus Christ. When we sit back and reflect on His birth and
subsequent death on the cross, we realize that there is no greater
gift known to mankind. God in His mercy sent His only begotten
Son to this earth (as 100 percent man and 100 percent God) to die
for the sins of this world. Christ willingly experienced a torturous
death in the depths of hell as a substitute for our Adamic sin nature, reconciling to Himself those who repent and accept by faith
the free gift of salvation. For Christians, the meaning of gift-giving
should have a special place in our hearts during this time of year.

Another compelling and powerful description of the true
spirit of giving is found in the book of Ruth. It relates a story of
how even the smallest of gift-giving gestures can turn into something that has lasting eternal value.

The Moabite widow, Ruth, was a kind and virtuous woman
who was dedicated to faithfully serving God. She also demonstrated an unwavering loyalty and commitment to her mother-in-
law, Naomi. Ruth left her native land of Moab (she was a Gentile)

with an uncommon zeal to minister to the needs of Naomi and serve God:

> And Ruth said, Entreat me not to leave thee, or to return from following after thee: for whither thou goest, I will go; and where thou lodgest, I will lodge: thy people shall be my people, and thy God my God. (Ruth 1:16)

After the untimely death of both her husband and two sons, Naomi decided to return to her native land and settle in Bethlehem. Ruth, who was widowed and childless herself, decided to accompany her mother-in-law on the long journey back. It was in the town of Bethlehem that Ruth experienced the graciousness of a wonderful and generous gift-giver named Boaz.

Boaz noticed Ruth as she was gleaning among the sheaves in the field (the law of Moses gave the poor the right to pick up crops left behind by the reapers). After further inquiry, he soon found out that Ruth had a reputation as a dedicated servant to Naomi, forsaking all that she had for lands unknown. Boaz noticed her kind and generous nature, disciplined work habits, and the trust that she exhibited in the Lord God of Israel:

> The Lord recompense thy work, and a full reward be given thee of the Lord God of Israel, under whose wings thou art come to trust. (Ruth 2:12)

Boaz was not content for this poor (but righteous) servant of God to simply glean around the edges like most of the poor. He instructed his young men to let other portions of the crop fall among the sheaves so Ruth could gather those as well. He wanted to help her out so that she could reap an extra measure of barley. Boaz wanted his men to purposefully (handfuls of purpose) let fall to the ground an additional portion of the crop:

And let fall also some of the handfuls of purpose, for
her, and leave them, that she may glean them, and rebuke her not. (Ruth 2:16)

What a wonderful depiction of a generous gift-giver. Boaz
was someone who noticed the needs of another servant of the
Lord and took action. When is the last time you went the extra
mile to give someone "handfuls of purpose?" When is the last
time you moved beyond the common and traditional forms of
gift-giving to something so special that it couldn't go unnoticed
or unrecognized? What will you do next Christmas to indicate
that you understand the power and the value of purposeful gift-
giving?

Well, for all of you romantics out there, I know what you are
thinking. You are saying to yourself, "Wait a minute, Boaz ended
up marrying Ruth, right?" You're also thinking, "Isn't that the ultimate gift in this narrative from the book of Ruth?" Okay, you
got me! You are correct. In the end, Boaz does decide to do the
right thing and redeems the inheritance of Naomi, while ultimately taking Ruth as his wife.

However, that is not the end of this wonderful and amazing
story. What started as bestowing a simple gift of additional reap-
ing for Ruth was used by God in unimaginable ways with untold
blessings in the spiritual realm. What started as a small gift mor-
phed into a redemption of the field and a marriage union that
symbolizes Christ's work on the Cross of Calvary and love for His
church. It also symbolizes the reconciliation of both Jew (Boaz)
and Gentile (Ruth), as the marriage union became part of the line
of descendants to King David, through whom came Jesus Christ:

And Salmon begat Booz of Rachab; and Booz begat
Obed of Ruth; and Obed begat Jesse...
(Matt. 1:5)

And the women her neighbors gave it a name saying, There is a son born to Naomi; and they called his name Obed: he is the father of Jesse, the father of David. (Ruth 4:17)

In conclusion, gift-giving starts with noticing the needs of others while demonstrating selfless and authentic acts of kindness with no expectations in return. We do so as the Spirit of God consumes our hearts, minds, and souls. God may decide to multiply your gift-giving in ways not comprehensible by the human mind. Please be generous in your gift-giving to others at this time of year. Small gestures can be used in miraculous and eternal ways! Merry Christmas to all, and have a wonderful gift-giving season! Praise God!

11

FRANTICALLY SCURRYING

*With a bold, selfless, and uncompromising
determination, we eagerly set our face like flint to
proclaim and communicate the good news of Jesus
Christ our Lord.*

WHEN I SIT BACK and contemplate the cares, entanglements, and busyness of our Christian existence, I can't help but shake my head in utter dismay and unbelief. There is so much to do; so many people to see; and endless texts, emails, tweets, Facebook messages, and phone calls to answer that our pilgrimage and ambassadorship become dominated and controlled by them.

The endless onslaught of activity and distraction could fill the volumes of our individual life stories. We frantically scurry around from one event to another, soothing the human conscience that we have performed our duty once again. We fill up our days with worldly activities and expectations that allow us to check the boxes of accomplishment and victory. We proudly boast and expound the virtues of cramming so many things and so much "stuff" into our days! We become hypnotized with the adrenalin of activity composing our earthy existence. Oh, the pleasure and satisfaction of it all, we muse. This collection of life experiences will do little to extol the glory of His kingdom and the name of Jesus Christ, our Lord and Savior, if we are not deliberate, thoughtful, and focused.

> The fruit of the righteous is a tree of life; and he that winneth souls is wise. (Prov. 11:30)

Is the frantic scurrying that you are currently engaged in helping you bear righteous fruit for the tree of life? By contrast, are you frantically scurrying to win lost souls who are bound for an eternity in hell?

Most Bible-believing Christians fully understand that hell is a place of eternal torment and misery. In Luke 16, we read that hell is a place so scorched by the flames of eternal damnation that the rich man pleaded to have his brothers warned of his wretched condition. We also see that he cried to Father Abraham for mercy from the flames of death:

> And he cried and said, Father Abraham, have mercy on me, and send Lazarus that he may dip the tip of his finger in water, and cool my tongue; for I am tormented in this flame. (Luke 16:24)

> Then he said, I pray thee therefore, father, that thou wouldest send him to my father's house: For I have five brethren; that he may testify unto them, lest they also come into this place of torment. (Luke 16:27–28)

If we believe in a real and literal hell, why, then, aren't we frantically scurrying to tell others about the saving and redeeming knowledge of Jesus? Why aren't we testifying to family, friends, or anyone else that we meet, with a pronounced sense of urgency? For some, the answer is fear. For others, it could be faithlessness, self-centeredness, pride, lack of biblical understanding, or even addictive consumption with the pleasures of this world. Whatever the reasoning or rationale, we know that many Christians are not fulfilling their sacred responsibility.

The frantic scurrying that I am talking about is not some obnoxious and over-the-top process of evangelism. It is not a reckless abandon that does more spiritual harm than good. No! It is a deliberate, thoughtful, and focused process of reaching out with the gospel message to all those we encounter. The frantic scurrying that I envision encompasses much spiritual wisdom and discernment, along with a heart so concerned with the souls of men and women that they have no option but to act on their passion and zeal for others.

We need a Christlike compassion where we are moved to action by professing His name. We should never see the outward façade and exterior of human beings, but we should see souls and the need for Christ's life-changing message. We joyfully witness and testify in all of the earthly manifestations that God has provided here on earth.

When God tells us to "go ye therefore" I believe that we have a responsibility to proclaim His name in the cultural manifestations He has given us. We must be ready always to give an answer to those who need Jesus Christ. That need is not exclusive to a church building or even a family setting. God wants us to boldly proclaim His name wherever we are!

Will you renew your determination to proclaim Jesus Christ? Will you ask Christ to give you the passion and the zeal for lost souls? Will you frantically scurry around (deliberate, thoughtful, and focused process of evangelism) for the cause of Christ? Many of us have lost our way in the complex maze of earthly considerations. We have become numb and conditioned to the excessive "goings-on," with little-to-no regard for the weightier matters of spiritual significance. Please pray with me that Christians will once again turn to the Savior and the glorious responsibility of proclaiming His name!

12

ISRAEL THE CHOSEN

Pray for the peace of Israel.

THE SUN DOTH SHINE eternal on
the peculiar of the great I Am.
A blessed and jealous possession
of our Creator, Redeemer, and Friend.

A possession so weak and hardened now.
The apple of His eye are they still.
Unfortunate evidences of the enemy's work.
Will they run to seek God's will?

Steeped in heretical legalism,
their journey being derailed by lust.
Choosing to satisfy all fleshly desires,
for turning to God they must.

The lust of the eyes with pleasures fleeting
misguided as they may be,
brought worldly goods and entanglements much
as far as God's chosen could see.

Looking, wanting, and grasping
for the comforts of this earth,
is the best that man can conjure;

a void and spiritual dearth.

The pride-filled life so now engrained
a troublesome foothold they sought.
Seeking tradition and formality
The works of man's hands were bought.

An unfortunate end to a heavenly plan
God had no choice but to act.
Leaving now a mere remnant only
because of His promise and pact.

But what a responsibility we have
to love, adore, and to pray
for that sacred manifestation…His people.
Fresh desires, renewed beginnings, a new day.

Will ye rise all ye nations
to embrace the chosen … one and all?
Will ye rise in the face of adversity
to answer the Psalms, our duty, and call?

Hold nothing back press onward still
forsaking the world's demands.
Preserving our heritage against all odds
an alliance eternal … embracing their hand.

This poem depicts the sacred manifestation and instrumentality of a people who God chose to glorify Himself and point to a Savior. However, Israel is a nation so steeped in their Secular Humanist tradition and devices that only the love of a Creator God can sustain and confine their eternal existence to a heavenly spiritual home.

Pray for the peace of Jerusalem: they shall prosper that love thee. (Ps. 122:6)

13

HONORING GOD AS MASTER COMMUNICATORS

When the God of this universe willingly condescended to such a low degree by using mankind to communicate and herald the spiritual wonders of His enduring kingdom — Jesus Himself, it left us in a state beyond all intellectual comprehension.

DID YOU KNOW THAT God wants Christians to hone their communication skills to the point where they are considered master communicators? No way! Where do you see that in the Bible, you ask? Many of you reading this chapter have already started rationalizing all the reasons why you are not capable or even worthy of being assigned such a grand and visible commendation. All the "ya-but" excuses are ruminating around inside your head at this very moment. You may be thinking thoughts like: It is not my spiritual gift, I am not bent that way, I am just not comfortable in crowds, I am just not willing to go in that direction, I would rather stay in the background, I am better in one-on-one situations and prefer small groups.

When the God of this universe assigns us specific job responsibilities as believers, He expects our best. He expects that we will rise to the occasion and be the best communicators that we can be. For example, when He tells us in the *Great Commission* to "go ye therefore," Christ follows this up with the fact that He will be with us always even unto the end of the world (Matt. 28:19–20). When we are teaching and baptizing unbelievers in the name of the trinity, do you think there is one element of mediocrity in the assignment? No, there are high expectations (from the Spirit within) that we will thoroughly, passionately, and with expertise and skill tackle the most honorable of all earthly vocations. This can only be attempted if we are convinced that the Spirit of God demands our best. We can only give our best when we learn how to skillfully communicate, persuade, and build relationships with the lost and with each other.

> But sanctify the Lord God in your hearts: and be ready always to give an answer to every man that asketh you a reason of the hope that is in you with meekness and fear: (1 Pet. 3:15)

God also tells us *to love our neighbors* as ourselves. How will you love your neighbors as yourself if you don't even know them? How will you get to know them without the communication and relationship skills necessary to build an enduring trust? How will you build an enduring trust without exceptional and exemplary communication and relationship-building skills? But it is hard, you exclaim! It takes a lot of time, practice, and repetition to be comfortable in those situations, you grumble.

At the end of the day, that is where the rubber meets the road. Anything worth doing unto the Lord must be done in a spirit of excellence. God wants first place, not leftovers. He wants us to set our minds on accomplishing His tasks with the fervor and excellence demanded. We should NEVER concede that communicating and building relationships is of a secondary nature or nondescript pastime. That is simply not true. Becoming a master communicator is vital to our Christianity and in helping Christ build His kingdom.

What about our *mentoring and discipleship* responsibilities? Do you think that the degree of spiritual impact on others is commensurate with one's ability to genuinely and skillfully communicate and effectively build relationships? The answer is a resounding and unequivocal, yes! Keeping our mentees and those we disciple at arm's length with poor communication skills is a recipe for disaster. An uninformed and passive (mediocre) communication style does little to help build the solid Christian foundations needed for new believers or those we are counseling. It may allow one to check the box of a mentoring or discipleship opportunity but does little to develop the deep roots needed for godly counsel.

When I read the verse below, I see communication and relationship-building excellence. I see an excited, motivated, and spiritually discerned group of people building the kingdom of God through thoughtful and timely communication.

> And the things that thou hast heard of me among many witnesses, the same commit thou to faithful men, who shall be able to teach others also.
> (2 Tim. 2:2)

Will it cost us something? When we become (progressive in nature) master communicators for the glory of God, will it put us in a position of risk? Absolutely, 100 percent! Thank you, Lord, for allowing me the opportunity to be put at risk for the name of Christ. We, our family, relatives, and those in our inner circle will suffer persecution. Like Christ, we will be despised, rejected, and ostracized to the degree and level of our communication and relationship-building expertise. When the Lord gives us that level of wisdom and knowledge, we should expect a direct frontal assault from the world. In the Christian world, we should think of it as nothing more than sacrifice unto the Lord!

In Hebrews chapter 11, we see the diversity of faithful individuals that God used to effectively communicate a prophetic message of grace, love, and hope. I believe each of these individuals had the capacity to greatly influence others by understanding their communication roles. As a result, they were able to lead productive change for the Lord and impact the world. Those in the "Hall of Faith" had the trust and faith needed to exact real change for the Lord. Remember, our role and desire should be to influence others one conversation at a time. Christians are leaders by the very nature of their heavenly calling. Leaders learn how to communicate effectively. Master communicators also understand the intimacy of their responsibilities. There is no splash, only an understanding of the sacred roles (vocations) we are expected to execute.

That leads me to my final point of being a master communicator. As born-again believers, we yearn to understand His expectations for our lives. Lord, show me your will. Help me to understand the paths that you have paved. We plead with God to give us the answers to the following questions:

What do you want me to do? *Labor* unto the Lord.

What do you want me to say? *Communicate* unto the Lord.

How do you want me to act and behave? *Live* unto the Lord.

How can I honor you with every aspect of my life? *Sacrifice* unto the Lord.

We answer the call to each of those questions through faith, works, and the unrelenting spiritual sacrifices that please Him. But most importantly, we answer those questions with a mindset that we glorify God in everything that we do. There is another wonderful verse in Hebrews that supports that very line of thinking:

> But to do good and to communicate forget not: for
> with such sacrifices God is well pleased.
> (Heb. 13:16)

Yes, God is pleased with the sacrifices of our communication. Both the vertical (prayers) and horizontal (relationship building) aspects of communication are needed. We are also told in the verse above that we are not to forget to communicate to others.

14

OH, WRETCHED MAN THAT I AM

Sin is a wicked and evil oppression that consumes body, mind, and soul when we yield to its despicable temptations.

I AM SINFUL, BUT willing to daily die and mortify my sinful ways.

I am prideful, but willing to harness the desires of the abominable me.

I am a learned man, but willing to fall prostrate before the wisdom of my maker.

I am ignorant, but willing to open my mind to the choruses of God's Word.

I am Adam, but willing to passionately yearn for renewal and rebirth.

I am wrong, but willing to learn at the feet of my Master.

I am bitter, angry, and resentful, but willing to explore the depths of His great love and forgiveness.

I am melancholy, but willing to be lifted to heights unknown.

I am lustful, but willing to tame the urges of death.

I am a liar, but willing to choke back and drown the utterances of falsehood.

I am a wretched man, but willing to cry for the mercies of heaven.

I am a fool, but willing to seek the Christ of eternity.

I am duplicitous, but willing to yield to the narrow paths provided.

I am unloving, but willing to be changed in His Image.

I am weak, but willing to rest in that still small place of everlasting strength.

I am human, but willing to put on the righteousness of the Savior.

I am your adopted son and heir, and willing to forever demonstrate my ambassadorship, stewardship, and dominion responsibilities with humility.

I am a sinner, but willing through His sovereign power and grace to accept the free gift of salvation.

I am a Christian!

While the proclamations in this chapter were written to remind and challenge Christians of the ravaging effects of sin, they also help us consider the way of escape when we rest in the blood of Jesus Christ. The natural state of mankind is unlovely at its core, but when we accept Christ as our Savior, we become clean in His eyes!

15

REDEFINING HUMAN EXISTENCE

The world is redefining human existence when they walk out their earthly plight with a high-minded, prideful, and man-centered understanding of Creation.

THE SECULAR HUMANIST FORCES in our society are trying to re-define and reshape our culture. They are conditioning the minds of our youth to their terminology, standards, definitions, and overall understanding of what traditional values represent. Satan believes in reframing the Christian belief system with narratives (storytelling) that deconstruct the fundamental doctrines of our faith. He wants us to believe in new iterations of our faith, forsaking long-held fundamental and foundational truths.

For Satan, the old-fashioned gospel message is an affront and not enough. His followers want us to believe there is no right and wrong. They want everyone to operate in a relativistic "gray zone" void of absolute truth. The humanists are out to redefine EVERY element of what is pure, logical, natural, authoritative, and God-ordained. Simply put, they want to engender a chaotic and random view of the world by redefining human existence itself! Let us now look at how far they have come in the 21st century.

- Humanists have no bosses—only coworkers.
- Humanists have no parents—only peer-ents.

- Humanists have no winning and losing—only participation.
- Humanists have no traditional marriages—only what people define as marriage.
- Humanists have no authority—only chaos and confusion.
- Humanists have no order—only random selection.
- Humanists have no discipline—only "anything goes."
- Humanists have no absolute truth—only narrative to support a position.
- Humanists have no borders—only a country and global community that you define as one.
- Humanists have no traditional definition of integrity—only a philosophy of "keeping your word."
- Humanists have no traditional definition of authenticity—only a philosophy of "one void of any preconceived worldviews," i.e., Christian worldview.
- Humanists have no conformity—only disestablishmentarianism.
- Humanists have no worship—only passionate subordination to high-minded thinking.
- Humanists have no love—only self-indulgence.
- Humanists have no repentance—only manipulation to achieve desired and self-serving ends.
- Humanists have no origin—only the science of human engineering and discovery.
- Humanists have no sacrifice—only the desire and yearning for earthly advances.
- Humanists have no genders—only personages and identities of what one claims.
- Humanists have no God—only gods of humanity through enlightenment thinking and human reasoning.

REDEFINING HUMAN EXISTENCE

- Humanists have no hope of tomorrow—only an existence of the here and now.
- Humanists have no heaven—only the dark and dreary perspective of spiritual nothingness.
- Humanists have no joy—only entertainment and pleasure-seeking release.
- Humanists have no male instincts—only toxic masculinity with feminine overtures to contaminate God's order.
- Humanists have no respect for life—only the brutal murder of unborn children up to the day of their birth.

Does any of this sound familiar in our current culture? Does any of this concern you? Have we become so numb to their spiritual indoctrination that we are paralyzed and immobile? Are we no more than a dummied down spiritual version of ourselves, clinging to every vice and artifice of mankind? The progressive and anti-God factions in our country have done much in the last two decades to destroy what is good and right. As a country, when we look in the mirror, we are unrecognizable, to our detriment. The humanists see progress, while we see sin and iniquity. The humanists see a global community locked arm in arm, while we see Christ reigning on earth for a thousand years. They see an end, while we see the beginning of a glorious eternity filled with the essence of our Creator!

Let's once again use the verse below as the rallying cry and North Star for those Christians who seek to discern between good and evil in our society. As leaders, it should give us a clear path ahead. When we put on the mind of Christ with discerning wisdom, He will give us the door of utterance to combat everything contrary to His heavenly design.

Finally, brethren, whatsoever things are true, whatsoever things are honest, whatsoever things are just, whatsoever things are pure, whatsoever things are lovely, whatsoever things are of good report; if there be any virtue, and if there be any praise, think on these things. (Phil. 4:8)

Will you pray for our country? Will you pray for specific victory in moving our culture forward for the cause of Christ? Will you commit to intimate communion with our Sovereign Lord, begging Him to intercede on our behalf? Are you willing to stand up, shout from the rooftops, and, by the love and grace of God, tell the world, "Not on my watch?"

Redeeming the time, because the days are evil. (Eph. 5:16)

We must stand ready to discharge the totality of our righteous indignation on those who seek to distort and manipulate the holy nature of the Word of God. The culture must never be allowed to influence, redefine, or exact an alternative form of truth and godly living not found in the Bible.

16

THE JOY OF HOOP TRUNDLING

*Telling me stirs me to expand my thinking; showing me
allows me to see the demonstration of an experience;
chastening me allows me to grow in the wisdom of the
Lord through participation.*

THE CHILDHOOD GAME OF hoop trundling has been around for
many centuries and can be traced back to the days of ancient
Rome, Africa, Greece, Europe, and even the Byzantine Empire of
the first century. It was a terrific diversion for children and teen-
agers who needed to let off some steam; exert much of their pent-
up physical energy; compete by demonstrating their mastery of
the hoop trundling game; and fill the void of time and endless
boredom that often afflicts many young souls.[1] It is a game that
can be played by the poor and rich alike. The game knows no ra-
cial boundaries or geographical or economic constraints. If you
can find a nice round object that you can coax along a path, then
you are in the game! A simple wagon wheel, bicycle wheel, hula
hoop, or any round object that can be guided along with a stick
will suffice. While reading my daily devotions in the book of
Numbers, I was reminded that this childhood game has significant spiritual parallels for Christians of all ages.

In the game of hoop trundling, you first choose the wheel or
round object you'll use. Once selected, the wheel will be used for
the duration of the race. Similarly, hasn't God chosen us since the

foundation of the world? Hasn't He called us unto Himself without preference to race, creed, or color? By accepting that free gift of salvation, don't we also have the opportunity to run and finish the race while having eternal security in Him? He also tells us that He will never leave or forsake us.

> For whom he did foreknow, he also did predestinate to be conformed to the image of his Son, that he might be the first-born among many brethren. Moreover whom he did predestinate, them he also called: and whom he called, them he also justified: and whom he justified, them he also glorified." (Rom. 8:29–30)

> For whosoever shall call upon the name of the Lord shall be saved. (Rom. 10:13)

> I will not leave you comfortless: I will come to you. (John 14:18)

Subsequently, once your wheel has been identified and chosen, you must then gently propel and guide the wheel along the difficult path of the "obstacle course" that lies ahead. The "trundler" uses a stick to help the wheel remain on its proper course. When playing the game, the stick helps guide the hoop from the back, middle, sides, or even the front. Ultimately, you want to keep the hoop moving forward (on the path to success) on a surface void of rocks, potholes, or other impediments that will keep you from reaching your destination.

Once the wheel and the path have been selected, you then want to avoid looking back, making sure that you keep your eyes straight ahead. In the game of hoop trundling, looking back takes your focus off the road or pathway ahead, which could derail your efforts to win the race. You want to avoid crashing and burning in the race.

Likewise, Christ warns us not to look back and indulge our-selves in our former sinful ways. He wants us to put on the new man and walk in the newness of life. He doesn't want us to get distracted from the things that are pure, righteous, and holy. He wants us to look straight ahead for the joys and trials of the Chris-tian life which help shape our character.

> What shall we say then? Shall we continue in sin, that grace may abound? (Rom. 6:1)

> Knowing this, that our old man is crucified with him, that the body of sin might be destroyed, that hence-forth we should not serve sin. (Rom. 6:6)

Yes, there is a tremendous amount of navigation and care that goes into this hoop trundling endeavor. There are times when you simply tap and guide the hoop or wheel along its route, while at other times, more severe adjustments and guidance (while on the fly) are needed because of the treacherous terrain. Each move-ment and adjustment is made with an eye toward the prize. When we compare this to how God lovingly corrects and admonishes us, we begin to understand and relate to the fact that God is keep-ing us from much heartache and trouble with His guiding hand. He wants us to avoid the treacherous terrain of sin, iniquity, and strife. God has our best interests at heart and wants to conform us to the image of His Son—Jesus Christ. He also wants us to keep our eyes on the prize. Our God on high will give us the propor-tional guidance and correction needed to keep us on that narrow path to God's will.

> And we know that all things work together for good to them that love God, to them who are the called ac-cording to his purpose. (Rom. 8:28)

> I press toward the mark for the prize of the high call-
> ing of God in Christ Jesus. (Phil. 3:14)

When we think about both hoop trundling and our journey in life, each has forces that continue to narrow the way that leads us to victory! For the "trundler," he has the stick of gentle correction, guidance, and direction. He may even need to abruptly and aggressively make course corrections, if necessary. The "trundler" must stand ready to be in the exact position needed when correction is warranted. In the end, the hoop trundler who finishes the race gets to celebrate.

For the Christian, like the story of Balaam in the book of Numbers, the Lord will stand in our way to block our progress and chastise us if we are headed in the wrong direction. He will also narrow our way and limit our choices when He feels it is necessary. God our Father wants what is best for His children. He, too, stands ready to meet our every need. He is a God of love and will use whatever means necessary to get our attention and keep us on the narrow path of Christianity! A gentle and loving reminder, the complex circumstances of life, encouragement and wise counsel from fellow believers, and the convicting power of the Holy Spirit are all at His disposal for our spiritual maturation. We also learned in chapter 3 that He uses trials of affliction to help shape and grow us.

> And the angel of the LORD went further, and stood
> in a narrow place, where was no way to turn either to
> the right hand or to the left. (Num. 22:26)

Christian, are you looking straight ahead with an eye toward the prize or are you glancing over your shoulder to the sins of yesteryear? Are the potholes, rocks, and other impediments of life distracting you? Does it seem like you have lost your way and the rod of correction is vividly apparent? Is God standing in the way and narrowing your choices? If so, just ask a loving and generous

Savior for forgiveness, and allow the Word of God to consume your every thought! In so doing, God will illuminate His perfect will for your life. The exciting news for Christians is that God has prepared a place called heaven. When we finish the hoop trundling race of life, we get to rest in His holy presence and celebrate His glory! Amen!

---

[1] http://www.victoriana.com/antiquetoys/rollinghoop.html

17

THE BEATINGS OF SEPARATION

Judgement is left to the sole discretion of a holy and righteous God while reproof, rebuke, and godly chastisement (love) is within the purview of Christian responsibility as we engage in spiritual warfare, remembering to be clean before God and making sure that the motes within have been surgically removed and repaired.

I AM SO THANKFUL for fundamental (a.k.a. foundational) Christianity. Those believers who desire to live out the truths of the Bible with separated Christian lives are a blessing to me. For over 34 years, my wife and I have sat under the tutelage of dedicated fundamental pastors and men of God who have preached and lived out separated lives unto the Lord! Praise God for these wonderful Christian men!

We have also learned under their guidance and tutelage that we should never let down our guard on the separation front—not for one second. The discipline, desire, passion, and leading of the Holy Spirit should consume our determination to live separated lives to the very end. We hope and pray that one day in heaven we will hear those wonderful words, "Well done thou good and faithful servant." We practice separated living as an act of worship and praise as God (operative word—God) impresses upon our hearts the need for holy and righteous living. As God orchestrates the choruses and chords of progressive Christian sanctification in our lives, we *begin* to be molded and shaped into the perfect image of Christ.

However, I am also reminded that we should never be motivated for separation based on a long list of do's and don'ts that choke the leading and working of His Spirit. An improper motivation for Christian separation can lead us directly to the abyss of legalism and a works-based mentality that we discussed in the first chapter. In this chapter, I want to more fully explore what our motivation should be for helping and teaching others about separation along with some of the potential pitfalls and things to avoid.

> Brethren, if a man be overtaken in a fault, ye which are spiritual, restore such a one in the spirit of meekness; considering thyself, lest thou also be tempted. Bear ye one another's burdens, and so fulfill the law of Christ. For if a man think himself to be something, when he is nothing, he deceiveth himself. (Gal. 6:1–3)

> But speak thou the things which become sound doctrine: That the aged men be sober, grave, temperate, sound in faith, in charity, in patience. The aged women likewise, that they be in behavior as becometh holiness, not false accusers, not given to much wine, teachers of good things. (Titus 2:1–3)

We must be extremely careful not to beat people with the stick of righteous separation. If we are honest, I think that we can all think back to instances and circumstances in our lives where *we have led with the issues of separation first,* summarily pointing out with fervor the laundry list and inadequacies (sin issues) of growing Christians and inquiring unbelievers. We instinctively survey the landscape of those who are less mature in the faith, and we formulate in our minds the list of vices and areas of spiritual development and needed improvement. We have a natural tendency to want to jump right in, point out the sin, and fix the issues without even getting to know and love them as fellow believers in the Lord or love those who desperately need Him as Savior.

I believe there are many in fundamental circles who must learn to graciously and lovingly allow room for the Spirit of God to work. I believe that, by our very nature (the old man within), we have a propensity to commence with the conceptual spiritual beatings, vitriol, and judgment of the unsaved and those less mature in the Lord. On many occasions over the years, I have found myself rushing to righteous standards of judgment in the flesh, acting as if I were the divine lawgiver myself.

I am praying that all fundamental Christians (especially me) will desire to put away the whips, crown of thorns, and the scourging instruments of pharisaical judgment while putting on the peaceful and gentle edifice of love. Let us determine together to have a deeper understanding and love for fellow believers first before hastily rushing to the sin issues of "the law" and higher standards of righteous living.

Please do not misunderstand my intentions in pointing out the above approach. I believe the Bible and what it says about separation. All I am saying is that some of us need to readjust our attitudes and approaches when teaching, counseling, and encouraging those less mature in the faith. If we are unable or unwilling to make course corrections in our approach to Christian council along with a greater allowance for incremental growth (compared to the instant super-Christian expectations), I believe we will continue to see defections in our ranks to the more liberal factions of Christianity.

When we *first* learn to love people and get to know and respect them right where they are in their positions of life, then I believe that God will exponentially bless. When we develop compassion and love for the ungodly and not a spirit of judgment,

God will multiply our impact. If not, we will leave an unfathomable trail of resentment and bitterness in the wake of those pious and ceremonial beatings of separation.

In the present day and culture in which we live, I believe that the book of Acts clearly articulates a reasonable position and approach for a fundamental Christian teaching on separation. In their book, *Bringing Your Faith to Work*, Norman Geisler and Randy Douglas point out varied evangelistic approaches to spreading the gospel message. They indicate in the first half of Acts (1–12) that Peter is portrayed as the primary evangelistic leader. His primary approach to evangelism was a proclaimational style based on those he was engaged with at the time.

The Jews had a good grasp of who God was and had a general understanding of the Scriptures. Therefore, sharing the good news of the gospel through proclamation to the Jews was appropriate since they could connect the dots to a coming Messiah. However, in the second half of Acts (13–28), the Apostle Paul was the primary evangelistic leader and used a totally different approach. Paul was dealing with a Roman-Greek culture who knew little about God and the Scriptures. Paul used much more of a relationship-oriented approach to proclaiming the gospel message.

Shouldn't we be taking a page out of that same divine playbook in the book of Acts when counseling on separation? We are living in a day and age where many people have limited knowledge and understanding of God's Word. We once had a Christian consensus in our society where Christian values were shared by believers and unbelievers alike. That isn't the case anymore. We are in an age where the secular humanist consensus has taken root.

Shouldn't we adjust our approach on separation with those we are trying to reach? Shouldn't our counsel and guidance on separation first begin with genuine love and concern (relationship-oriented) for others while building long-lasting friendships in the Lord? I do not believe that preaching **at** people and pointing out all their sin issues will create the trust needed to help people grow in the Lord.

I would like to use a few humorous (reverse illustrations) captions to make my point relating to a gracious and loving approach on the issue of separation.

> The beatings will continue until your attitude about separation changes.

> I am going to slap you upside your head if you don't start practicing righteous separation.

> If all you are is the separation hammer, everything will look just like a nail.

As Christians, we are called to be separate and distinct in our approach to living out our faith here on earth. There is no debate on that issue. However, it is the Holy Spirit who will work in the lives of Christians everywhere, bringing them closer to His image and standards of excellence. And yes, Christ will use us as instruments and channels to guide and direct.

Why do we often lead with separation in our discipleship? Why do we want to bring out the checklist items of separation before we even get to know them? Why are we so obsessed with "hammering" people into compliance for doing all the right things while the rest of the Bible gets lost, overlooked, or becomes secondary? I want to offer a few simple explanations for us to consider.

- **Some Christians are exuberant** – These Christians are so full of zeal and exuberance for the Lord that they overwhelm the less spiritually grounded (they cast an inadvertent cloud of demanding compliance).

- **Some Christians are fearful** – These Christians are inadequately trained and are afraid they will not be able to provide the proper guidance and counsel for sin issues (easier to stay in their comfort zones by telling others what not to do).
- **Some Christians are lazy** – These Christians are predisposed to pointing out and proclaiming what should be corrected vs. engaging in meaningful teaching moments from the Word of God (teaching is hard work, and they prefer not to get involved).
- **Some Christians are novices** – These Christians treat their salvation experience as a badge of honor and have a "secret club" mentality where the rules must be obeyed (a religious club compared to a dynamic and living faith in God).
- **Some Christians are prideful** – These Christians take much pleasure in the sanctimonious and royal decrees that others are not living for the Lord (they think they have achieved a higher-level understanding and discernment with an air of superiority).
- **Some Christians have blind spots** – These Christians are so hard-wired toward the issues of separation that they "can't see the forest through the trees."

Ultimately, we need to get to know people and learn how to genuinely love them. We must ask the Spirit of God to give us a profound and unselfish motivation to lovingly and gently guide people to new spiritual heights. Yes, we are to hate sin. Fortunately for us, Christ has died for the ungodly and was the sacrifice and propitiation for the sins of the world. Let us desire to put away the dogmatic, uncompromising, and judgmental sword of separation, replacing it with the sweet aroma of spiritual discernment and grace. Praise God in the highest!

18

GOD'S STRENGTH

There is no such community of kindred souls and like-minded brethren as when one desires to step forth into the holiest of holies following the call of a righteous Savior and becoming citizens of His heavenly body of believers.

GOD'S STRENGTH COMES NOT in activities we do,
Nor covenant sacrifices performed for you.
God's strength comes not from internal might,
For the Bible says those things take flight.

God's strength comes not from emotional claim,
But through the narrow and heavenly way.
God's strength comes not in this world's gain,
But in humble submission to His wonderful name.

God's strength comes not from the music we play,
Nor from the works that we perform each day.
God's strength comes not from buildings and things,
Nor large crowds, man-made efforts to bring.

God's strength comes not through winds of change,
But through His nature which remains the same.
God's strength comes not from prideful eyes,

But through Christ Jesus who was willing to die.

God's strength does come to the obedient man,
Who rests in the divine and foundational plan.
God's strength does come to those who wait,
Anticipating His coming, our glorious fate.

God's strength does come when we seek His face,
Desiring salvation for the lost human race.
God's strength does come when yielded to Him,
Fleeing the old man's wretched iniquity and sin.

God's strength does come when the Spirit indwells,
For now we are Christians, a godly legacy to tell.
God's strength does come when motivated by love,
An agape existence given from on-high up above.

19

INSIDE THE FOUR WALLS

Government officials who don't have a personal
relationship with Jesus Christ and who are informed by
their secular humanist philosophies on life are making
policy decisions in the flesh... The Supreme Court has
ruled on several occasions that Secular Humanism is an
organized religion

THERE HAS BEEN MUCH talk within fundamental Christian circles along with a group of mainstream conservative political commentators that says our First Amendment rights could be greatly jeopardized in the years and decades ahead. At the very least, they say, our religious rights could be severely curtailed and limited to the four walls of a church building.

Our religious freedoms could be limited to worshipping our Lord and Savior within the confines of the church building itself. Anything beyond this (witnessing, evangelism, and other forms of so-called proselytizing) may be regarded as discriminatory or considered a hate crime to those who do not share our beliefs.

They argue that adherence to Christian values in the marketplace will be shunned, looked down upon, and recognized as unlawful in the future. Some believe that evangelicalism and fundamentalism (foundationalism) will be discarded because Christians will fear legal retribution in the marketplace and cower to their demands.

It also appears, based on recent rulings, that the argument is true and is being played out across America today! Currently, laws are being enacted that are directly opposed to God's principles. Any legislation that would require us to submit to anti-God laws (defined as laws that force us to contradict our deeply held scriptural beliefs) and a Supreme Court that could be activist in nature instead of taking an "originalist" view of interpreting the constitution is worrying.

An activist court would be in a position to enforce the anti-God pieces of legislation described above. A combination of these two factors would be disastrous to the religious landscape of America for generations to come. We are already seeing evidences of this phenomenon in numerous legal proceedings around the country.

Small businesses and other Christian entities in the marketplace are being told to conform to the anti-God laws of the land, or else. If they don't, the government will fine them, shut their organization down (one way or another), send them to jail, or potentially all of the above. This is a chilling and concerning environment for fundamental Christians who want to actively live out their faith in the marketplace according to biblical commands and precepts.

What ever happened to the notion of limited government? In the verses below, we have clear biblical mandates that we should obey God first, rather than man, and render unto God the things that are God's:

> Then Peter and the *other* apostles answered and said, We ought to obey God rather than men. (Acts 5:29)

> They say unto him, Caesar's. Then saith he unto them, Render therefore unto Caesar the things which are Caesar's; and unto God the things that are God's. (Matt. 22:21)

So, what will you do in the months and years ahead? When laws are enacted that force you to choose between obeying man or obeying God, who will you choose? Will you stay true to God's Word or will you find a *convenient way to rationalize your acceptance of the world's "new normal?"* How committed will you be when push comes to shove? In addition to the Bible, the laws of the land as described in the First Amendment to our Constitution by our forefathers seem to be clear cut as well. Congress can't make any laws that prohibit the free exercise of religion. End of story, or is it?

Congress adopted the First Amendment in 1791, and it reads as follows:

> *Congress shall make no law respecting an establishment of religion, or prohibiting the free exercise thereof;* or abridging the freedom of speech, or of the press; or the right of the people peaceably to assemble, and to petition the Government for a redress of grievances.[1]

Isn't that what many of the recent laws that have been passed are forcing us to do? They prohibit the free exercise of our deeply held religious beliefs. They force us to obey man rather than God. For example, we are being forced to accept a redefinition of marriage that is contrary to the Word of God and are forced to provide marketplace patronage to those who violate our religious liberty of conscience.

Our government is passing laws that are in direct conflict with our religious convictions and is forcing a showdown of the highest magnitude. This issue is also showing itself in corporations across America. Christians are being forced to adopt corporate policies that are in direct opposition to their religious beliefs. In the future, it will almost be impossible for fundamental Christians to rise to the top of corporate organizations, *outside of pandering to their social causes under the shadow and cover of "inclusivity."* As this issue explodes across the United States, all one has to do is "follow the money" to find out where it will land next. When there is money at stake, there will be a pandering to the world's agenda. Ultimately, it will be the difference between obeying God and obeying man. Rationalize as you will, but those are the facts!

Many of the arguments we hear about the infringement of religious liberty seem to make sense, except for one. Historically, we have looked to those on the opposing side of the religious liberty issue and have consequently laid the blame at their feet. It is their fault. It is those who are driving the anti-God agendas that we should blame. I take exception to this. There is no other place we should look except to ourselves. The religious liberty issue rests squarely on our shoulders.

As a Christian nation and body of believers, if we feel laws are being passed that are an affront to our beliefs, then we should rise up and do something about it. We should not sit back and blame others for what we have allowed and indirectly helped create. We should not throw our hands in the air and just be satisfied that the course of America (the Bible tells us that the end times are coming) will take place with or without our direct involvement. Make no mistake— this is our collective mess.

As a Christian nation, we have sat idly by and watched from afar the progress of Satan and his minions on this issue. We have been content in the secure confines of our homes, with material abundance, to cast a blind eye to the fiery darts of Satan. Christian, this is your country. What are you going to do about it? Will you do every lawful thing possible on the front end of this issue before the ultimate moments of truth come? If you do not act now, there will soon be a time when you will be forced to choose. Will you make the necessary adjustments and provisions now to stop the encroachment of Satan on the lands of America?

As a Church, what do you think would happen in America if we voiced our collective displeasure about anti-God legislation? I believe that the politicians and power brokers in this great country would melt faster than Frosty the Snowman. They would fall prostrate before an Almighty God, acknowledging the power of the Holy Spirit and the decisiveness of the horizontal covenant relationship among Christian believers. They would try to hold on to their power bases like a cowboy does when riding a bucking bronco. As a Christian nation, we must act—this is our duty! How will we be able to fulfill the Great Commission's directives if our evangelical voices are silenced?

> Go ye therefore, and teach all nations, baptizing them in the name of the Father, and of the Son, and of the Holy Ghost: Teaching them to observe all things whatsoever I have commanded you: and, lo, I am with you always, even unto the end of the world. (Matt. 28:19–20)

A. W. Tozer made three distinct statements that I believe support the narrative in this article.

> People think of the world, not as a battleground, but as a playground. We are not here to fight; we are here to frolic. We are not in a foreign land; we are at home. We are not getting ready to live, but we are already living, and the best we can do is rid ourselves of our inhibitions and our frustrations and live this life to the full.
>
> But when whole regiments of professed believers are too timid to fight and too smug to be ashamed, surely it must bring an astringent smile to the face of the enemy; and it should bring a blush to the cheeks of the whole Church of Christ.
>
> The average Christian today is a harmless enough thing. God knows. He is a child wearing with considerable self-consciousness the harness of the warrior; he is a sick eaglet that can never mount up with wings; he is a spent pilgrim who has given up the journey and sits with a waxy smile trying to get what

pleasure he can from sniffing the wilted flowers he has plucked by the way.[2]

Christians should be resolute in not allowing our Christian faith to be painted inside the boundaries of the four walls of a church building. If allowed, the very foundation of our great country will be changed forever. Satan is clever, and he is currently experimenting with alternative ways to shut down our Christian voices. We can't let this happen!

So what do we do? We must fully utilize the second half of the First Amendment to the Constitution of the United States to let our voices be heard.

> ... or abridging the freedom of speech, or of the press; or the right of the people peaceably to assemble, and to petition the Government for a redress of grievances.[3]

- Voice your opinions.
- Utilize the press.
- Call your politicians at the state, local, and federal level.
- Assemble peaceably.
- Petition the government.
- Never stop being engaged in the political process.
- Vote for those who you feel will best represent our country.

Please pray that God will work miracles in the hearts of American Christians and beyond. Amen!

[1] https://www.law.cornell.edu/constitution/first_amendment

[2] A. W. Tozer, *Tozer For the Christian Leader*, Compiled by Ron Eggert, (Chicago: Moody Publishers, 2015).

[3] https://www.law.cornell.edu/constitution/first_amendment

20

Unmoving, Unchanging, Always

Atonement is the selfless act of reconciliation and a loving sacrifice.

IN LUKE CHAPTER 4, the Word of God gives us a stark contrast between the motivation and mindset of Satan compared to the heavenly and eternal focus of Jesus Christ. The great tempter (Satan) enacted a full-court press with untold veracity on the Lord in the wilderness. From these great trials (with an ensuing victory), we further glean a true understanding and appreciation for the selfless, righteous, and loving character of our Savior. Christ's character during the temptation was so focused and resolute to the will of the Father that Satan himself had to realize the depth and breadth of an unmoving, unchanging, and always present obedient spirit in Christ.

> Being forty days tempted of the devil. And in those days did he eat nothing: and when they were ended, he afterward hungered. (Luke 4:2)

One can only imagine the intensity and aggressive nature of the attacks from Satan. Christ was tempted for 40 days by one of the most prominent and fallen angels that ever existed. Satan's clever, subtle, manipulative, and corrosive personality and evil spirit is active in trying to destroy everything that is good, holy, and righteous.

For His part in fending off the ruthless attacker, Christ decided to flee the physical needs of this world and took no food. My human instincts tell me that Christ wanted to bask in that still small place of God Almighty to be able to endure the onslaught of sin and oppression as He was being tempted in the wilderness by Satan.

This approach should not be lost on Christians everywhere. When we are under attack, do we flee the earthly pleasures and physical needs of this world in order to come under the complete and total control of God's Spirit?

As the chapter progresses, Satan now wants Christ to legitimize His standing as the Son of God. In other words, "Prove it to me. If you are as great and as powerful as you are made out to be, then prove it to me!"

> And the devil said unto him, If thou be the Son of God, command this stone that it be made bread. (Luke 4:3)

And while Satan could do nothing but focus on the earthly and material components of turning the stone into bread, Christ had a heavenly view full of spiritual discernment and focus that honored the one true God above. Yes, after 40 days in the wilderness without food, Christ was hungry. However, He would not give in to the evil manipulation:

> And Jesus answered him, saying, It is written, *that man shall not live by bread alone, but by every Word of God.* (Luke 4:4)

When Satan's tactic to entice the lust of the flesh was rendered of none effect by our Savior, Satan then moved to the lust of the eyes, showing Christ all the kingdoms of the world.

Through the eyes, Satan was hoping that Christ would covet the dominance and power of the world:

> And the devil, taking him up into a high mountain, showed unto him all the kingdoms of the world in a moment of time. And the devil said unto him, All this power will I give thee, and the glory of them: for that is delivered unto me; and to whomsoever I will I give it. (Luke 4:5, 6)

However, once again Christ rebuffed the advances of Satan by turning to the Lord. He would not let the allure and power of the world influence His determined obedience and servanthood:

> And Jesus answered and said unto him, Get thee behind me, Satan: for it is written, *Thou shalt worship the Lord thy God, and him only shalt thou serve.* (Luke 4:8)

Then, in a final attempt to sway and tempt Jesus, Satan had a plan to tickle the prideful (pride of life) and self-aggrandizing character of the Lord—should there be any. Satan played on the fact that Christ could command legions of angels should He so desire. However, Christ would have none of it as He pointed back to the Lord in His response:

> And he brought him to Jerusalem, and set him on a pinnacle of the temple, and said unto him, If thou be the Son of God, cast thyself down from hence: For it is written, *He shall give his angels charge over thee, to keep thee: and in their hands they shall bear thee up, lest at any time thou dash thy foot against a stone.* (Luke 4:9–11)

Christ understood that to be obedient to God meant being obedient to the agony of the Cross. No amount of power, influence, or physical/material abundance would stop Him from fulfilling His destiny on the Cross of Calvary. Christ clearly had to wrestle with the profound extremities of the following desires:

> For all that is in the world, the lust of the flesh, and the lust of the eyes, and the pride of life, is not of the Father, but is of the world. (1 John 2:16)

What a spectacular picture we have of an unmoving, unchanging, and always present obedient spirit in Christ Jesus. Even amid unimagined spiritual temptation, we see that we serve a Savior that was obedient to the Cross. His great love for us knows no limits or bounds. Praise God!

> Jesus Christ the same yesterday, and to day, and for ever. (Heb. 13:8)

21

SECOND FIDDLE IS OKAY

*Unity demands forbearance, humility, and the
demonstrated love of God Almighty even when we don't
feel like it.*

WE ARE TOLD AS Christian leaders that we need to have a relent-
less drive, determination, discipline, resilience, passion, and overall "stick-to-a-tive-ness" (among numerous other leadership
character traits) to be the best that we can be. As Christians, we
should give it our all and rise to the top of our respective fields of
endeavor for God's glory. In the workplace, it may mean aspiring
to be president or chief executive officer of a major corporation.
We think to ourselves, "If I could only rise to this level of authority I could have much more of an impact for the Lord."

In a ministry setting, it may mean being the pastor of a large
church with a congregation of tens of thousands. The preacher's
desire may be to build an enormous organization and reach as
many people as possible for Christ.

In the athletic arena, it may mean striving to be the most valuable player (MVP) on the team or leading your teammates in all
the offensive and defensive statistical categories. Day after day,
athletes go to the practice field and hone their crafts to become
professionals and be the best in their respective sport. Christian
athletes believe they have been given this God-given natural ability and want to use it for His glory!

We want to be the best! But what happens in each of these areas when you come up short of these tall aspirations? What happens when all the planning and hard work doesn't get you to the so-called ideal place in life? What happens when you do not reach the summit of all your goals, plans, and dreams? Think for a moment—what if God wants you in a backup role and wants you to play second fiddle to help pave the way for others? How will you respond?

While exploring this topic, there are three primary considerations that will be discussed, using the Bible as our guide. First, we will look at some Bible characters of the early Christian church along with key Old Testament figures and how they responded. Second, I would like to evaluate the *second fiddle* syndrome from what God has to say about the use of our spiritual gifts. Third, this article will discuss the impact that God's timing has in all of this. Taken collectively, I believe that God has given us a proper framework to discuss and think through this topic.

John the Baptist

This is one of my all-time favorite Bible characters. John the Baptist was called to pave the way for our Lord and Savior, Jesus Christ. God asked him to play second fiddle, and he did it with joy! John made three statements that epitomized who he was as a follower of Christ:

> He said, I am the voice of one crying in the wilderness, make straight the way of the Lord, as said the prophet Isaiah. (John 1:23)

> He it is, who coming after me is preferred before me, whose shoe's latchet I am not worthy to unloose. (John 1:27)

This is he of whom I said, After me cometh a man which is preferred before me: for he was before me. And I knew him not: but that he should be made manifest to Israel, therefore am I come baptizing with water. (John 1:30–31)

What makes John's comments so special was his selfless perspective and his willingness to declare the preference of someone else before himself. In human terms, what he was communicating runs counter to the natural predisposition of most human beings. Let's pause to think about the historical context for a minute. John had notoriety, followers (disciples), and the attention of the government officials. He was an enigma and people wanted to be around him and hear what he had to say. John's message was having an impact on people's lives. Many of his followers believed that he was a prophet and on the same spiritual plane with Elijah. His ministry was also growing in popularity. There were droves of converts and other disciples coming to John for baptism as he preached a message of repentance. Jesus himself came to John to be baptized. There was even a time period where John's ministry overlapped the ministry of Christ.

So what did John do? Did he capitalize on his growing fame to make himself the center of attention? Did he move to more populated urban areas where the opportunity for additional fame and glory awaited him? No, he did not! John understood that his call from the Lord meant playing *second fiddle* and paving the way for his Lord. He preached in the wilderness, ate locusts and honey, and was content with the role that the Lord provided for him. He was unwilling to take advantage of his situation for the furtherance of self. Rather, John knew that the best that he could be was to proclaim the coming of a Savior and by his willingness to *"make straight the way of the Lord."* His was a generous and selfless act for the glory of God.

Apostle Paul

Unlike John the Baptist, who was growing in popularity in a remote region, the Apostle Paul had already achieved the highest levels of leadership impact and influence in society at large. In today's terms, Paul would have been considered an influential star, mover-and-shaker, and at the top of his game. He was a Roman citizen, studied at the feet of Gamaliel (who was a well-known intellectual of the day), and was recognized by the ruling elite as a person of influence and power. Paul sums up his credentials—in the world's eyes— in a couple of verses:

> Circumcised the eighth day, of the stock of Israel, of the tribe of Benjamin, a Hebrew of the Hebrews; as touching the law, a Pharisee; Concerning zeal, persecuting the church; touching the righteousness which is in the law, blameless. (Phil. 3:5–6)

Wow! Paul was the real deal! He couldn't have come from any better lineage or stock than that described above. However, like John the Baptist, the Apostle Paul was willing to lay down his life for the sake of the gospel. He, too, parted ways with the allurements of this present world to embark on a lifelong commitment to the Lord:

> But what things were gain to me, those I counted loss for Christ. Yea doubtless, and I count all things but loss for the excellency of the knowledge of Christ Jesus my Lord: for whom I have suffered the loss of all things, and do count them but dung, that I may win Christ. (Phil. 3:7–8)

So there it was—Paul's willingness to play second fiddle to a cause much greater than himself, the cause of Christ.

King David

Here sat a king with a heavenly anointing from above who was considered a man after God's own heart! David was a young shepherd boy who slew the giant Goliath, was anointed king by Samuel, had legions of followers, and eventually unified and consolidated power in the Northern and Southern Kingdoms. By the world's standards, he was a dominant political and religious powerhouse who had the authority, charisma, leadership capabilities, and legitimacy to rule his countrymen. Yet, when David had the chance to slay his nemesis, King Saul (who repeatedly tried to destroy him), he instead chose a path that would put him in a position of second fiddle until God's timing was evident. He would not usurp the position of King Saul:

> And David said to Abishai, Destroy him not: for who can stretch forth his hand against the Lord's anointed, and be guiltless? (1 Sam. 26:9)

David's restraint in not killing or removing King Saul from the throne and immediately consolidating power when he had the opportunity to do so was an incredible testimony to his relationship with the Lord. David was so in tune with the Lord's will for his life at this point that he would not "stretch forth his hand against the Lord's anointed." He was content abiding in the wilderness and being on the run from King Saul until the Lord's perfect timing. David had such a respect for God's anointed king (Saul) that when David "cut off the skirt of Saul's robe privily," he was upset with himself for being disrespectful.:

> And the men of David said unto him, Behold the day of which the Lord said unto thee, Behold, I will deliver thine enemy into thine hand, that thou mayest do to him as it shall seem good unto thee. Then David arose, and cut off the skirt of Saul's robe privily. And

it came to pass afterward that David's heart smote him, because he had cut off Saul's skirt. And he said unto his men, The Lord forbid that I should do this thing unto my master, the Lord's anointed, to stretch forth mine hand against him, seeing he is the anointed of the Lord. (1 Sam. 24:4–6)

In lieu of the circumstances, David was even willing to refer to King Saul as master! What a wonderful testimony of loyalty and respect.

Joshua

In many respects, we find a description of the wonderful blessings of being placed in a role of *second fiddle* with the account of Joshua, Moses' minister. For decades, Joshua stood at his leader's side in a less prominent role only to be used greatly of the Lord in the future. Joshua served at Moses' command during the exodus period, two wilderness odysseys, and eventually during the conquest of the Promised Land. One can only imagine the wealth of knowledge and wisdom he learned at Moses' side. What an awesome spiritual training ground! Yes, it was the servant Joshua who was second-in-command that God eventually commissioned to cross the Jordan River and conquer the lands:

Now after the death of Moses the servant of the LORD it came to pass, that the LORD spake unto Joshua the son of Nun, Moses' minister, saying, "Moses my servant is dead; now therefore arise, go over this Jordan, thou, and all this people, unto the land which I do give to them, even to the children of Israel." (Josh. 1:1–2)

Can you think of anyone more qualified to lead the crossing of the Jordan River than Joshua? His unique position as second fiddle in the previous decades allowed him the time to listen, learn, let go, live, and lead. Joshua had the God-given experiences, wisdom, credentials, and understanding to take on the challenges awarded him! The "proving ground" under Moses' leadership was like none other and fully prepared him for the task at hand. Joshua understood the people of Israel and their inclinations and he understood God's promise while having the fervor and discipline to get the job done. Oh, that the Lord would allow me an opportunity like Joshua to be *second fiddle* for the cause of Christ! Praise the Lord!

Our Spiritual Gifts

The Bible clearly articulates the diversity of spiritual gifts. We have all been gifted with unique and distinguishable gifts and talents that are to be used for His service. A church is fully functioning when EVERYONE is using their spiritual gifts to the fullest extent, with joy. Anything less and there is a chink in the armor of the local body of believers. Let's see what the book of 1 Corinthians has to say on this subject.

> Now there are diversities of gifts, but the same Spirit. And there are differences of administrations, but the same Lord. And there are diversities of operations, but it is the same God which worketh all in all. But the manifestation of the Spirit is given to every man to profit withal. For to one is given by the Spirit the word of wisdom; to another the word of knowledge by the same Spirit; To another faith by the same Spirit; to another the gifts of healing by the same Spirit; To another the working of miracles; to another prophecy; to another discerning of spirits; to another divers kinds of tongues: to another the interpretation of

tongues: But all these worketh that one and the self-same Spirit, dividing to every man severally as he will. (1 Cor. 12:4–11)

But what does this have to do with the topic of *second fiddle*? Let's think about it from an exaggerated point of view. Using the examples at the beginning of this chapter, what would organizational life look like if everyone was the CEO or president? Do you think things would get accomplished? How about all those details that most executives can't stand? What would happen to them? Outside of lofty thinking and strategy discussions, who would actually do the so-called "grunt" work?

On the other hand, what would the ministry look like if preachers only served and ministered to large congregations? Who would minister to those who live in rural areas? What would happen to the local body of believers? What would happen if all the players on a major-league baseball team's roster were catchers? How do you think the team would function? It seems to me that there would be a bunch of confusion and turmoil. There would be no pitchers, fielders, or those that could run the bases with speed. There would be no one who could run down those long fly balls in the outfield.

Well, I am sure that you get the point by now. Everyone has a job to do and a spiritual gift(s) to exercise. Everyone can't sit at the top of an organizational pyramid. However, what everyone can do is be at the top of their game for the glory of God. We need to be good stewards and be content with the roles and responsibilities God has afforded us. It should be a privilege to serve the God of this universe in a capacity of *second fiddle*.

Timing

I would be remiss if I didn't touch on the Lord's perfect timing in our lives. In today's fast-pasted American culture, our citizens have everything at their fingertips. They have access to most anything, and they can get it right away. There is no waiting around. With a few clicks of a button, we can gain access to most of life's needs and wants. However, I do not believe that the Lord is in all of that. This is the world's system and its view of how things should be done. It wants us to compete against one another, covet one another's possessions, and never be satisfied or content with our station in life. In its eyes, more is always better.

I believe the obsession with "me" and "now" is destroying the benefits of lifelong learning. We want to skip over all the key learning moments of life to get what we want—right away. There is no doubt in my mind that God puts us in a position of second fiddle for our development. He wants to mold us into His image. Oftentimes, he has to slow down our aspirations to make sure we understand that He is in control. This allows us the opportunity to experience life, learn patience, be content, grow spiritually, and then learn to fly. It really is okay to be second fiddle. It is okay to slow down, relax, take time to smell the roses, and allow God to put you in the positions in life that are best for your eternal development. For all the overachievers and type "A" personalities out there, this message is for us.

In summary, we are on an exciting, awe-inspiring, and unimaginable journey here on earth for the glory of God. Our Heavenly Father has adopted us into His family and wants what is best for His children. He will allow situations to mold, guide, and instruct us along the way. His will for our lives is perfect. We need to stop and hear the still small voice of our Creator. We need to learn to appreciate and enjoy each step of the journey. And while the world may tell us a much different story, *second fiddle* is okay! May the Lord help us strive to be our best in the positions of life He has placed us and where He is allowing us to grow spiritually. Amen!

22

MOMENTS OF TRUTH

Fear ensues when the planned controls of one's life give way to an alternative manifestation of functional spiritual reality, pushing mankind to cower in the corner at its loss.

For I came down from heaven, not to do mine own will, but the will of him that sent me. (John 6:38)

The Jews then murmured at him, because he said, I am the bread which same down from heaven. (John 6:41)

Verily, verily, I say unto you, He that believeth on me hath everlasting life. (John 6:47)

I am the living bread which came down from heaven: if any man eat of this bread, he shall live forever: and the bread that I will give is my flesh, which I will give for the life of the world. (John 6:51)

Many therefore of his disciples, when they had heard this, said, This is a hard saying; who can hear it? (John 6:60)

From that time many of his disciples went back, and walked no more with him. Then said Jesus unto the 12, Will ye also go away? (John 6:66–67)

After these things Jesus walked in Galilee: for he would not walk in Jewry, because the Jews sought to kill him. (John 7:1)

THERE ARE HUNDREDS AND even thousands of decision-points in our lives where the paths we take and the roads we travel will have lasting spiritual and eternal significance. The Cambridge English Dictionary defines a moment of truth as "an occasion when something important happens that tests someone or something and that will have an effect on the future."[1] These moments of truth will lay the foundation for the type of Christian we aspire to be and the impact that we want to have on friends, family, and acquaintances. These specific moments of truth are all turning points in our lives that could potentially bring us to elevated spiritual heights or point us in a direction that will lead to destruction. If not total destruction, it will lead us to a place where we will be much less usable for the Lord our God. It will limit our leadership capabilities and influence for His optimal service in the long run.

For example, think back to that moment when we asked Christ to save our soul! What a miraculous point in our spiritual development and the ultimate turning point in our eternal destiny. When God called us to a saving knowledge of His Son and we accepted that free gift of salvation, our perspective on life took on a whole new meaning. We began to form habits and live our lives in ways that ran contrary to the world and its thinking. We started to read our Bibles, pray, worship, attend church, and associate with like-minded Christians in the faith. Spiritually speaking, our world was turned upside down. The way we think, act, and relate to the world should now be tempered by the Word of God.

That one point in time; that one decision; that one perfect moment of truth determined our eternal courses in both the physical and spiritual worlds. Praise the Lord! What about all the other moments of truth you encounter as ambassadors for Christ? How are you handling them? Are you shrouding your fundamental Christian testimonies with the cloaks of righteousness and purity? Are you leading? What specific action items will you put in place right now for the glory of God? Are you P.R.O.U.D. of what it means to be a fundamental Christian?

> **P** – Proving what is the good and acceptable will of God
> **R** – Ringing out the good news of the gospel message
> **O** – Offering your life as a sweet savor unto the Lord; without blemish
> **U** – Unifying the brethren by the giving of your tithes, talents, and time
> **D** – Defending the doctrines of the faith

When surveying the first four books of the New Testament, it is no surprise that we find contrasting and somewhat paradoxical descriptions of how Bible characters reacted during defining moments of truth. Yes, these Bible characters were some of the so-called early Christian leaders in the establishment of the church. Many were out front and leading the way, while others were standing and watching as events unfolded. Please remember that these early Christian leaders were human beings just like you and me. They had fears, worries, and inhibitions like the ones we have today. These leaders were sinners saved by the grace of God. It was a point in history when Christ walked the face of this earth and declared that He was the Savior! This was an unpopular and revolting message for many, to be sure.

> For I came down from heaven, not to do mine own will, but the will of him that sent me. (John 6:38)

The Jews then murmured at him, because he said, I am the bread which same down from heaven. (John 6:41)

Verily, verily, I say unto you, He that believeth on me hath everlasting life. (John 6:47)

I am the living bread which came down from heaven: if any man eat of this bread, he shall live forever: and the bread that I will give is my flesh, which I will give for the life of the world. (John 6:51)

Many therefore of his disciples, when they had heard this, said, This is a hard saying; who can hear it? (John 6:60)

From that time many of his disciples went back, and walked no more with him. Then said Jesus unto the 12, Will ye also go away? (John 6:66–67)

After these things Jesus walked in Galilee: for he would not walk in Jewry, because the Jews sought to kill him. (John 7:1)

In the verses above, Christ declared that He was equal with God. The Jewish ruling elite took great exception to His proclamation and wanted to silence and ultimately destroy Him. However, even more disturbing were the actions of those believing disciples who identified themselves with Christ. They were supposed to be leading the charge and "taking the hill" for the Lord. Unfortunately, those Christian disciples had a moment of truth, and "walked no more with him." For whatever reason, they did not have the courage, faith, or depth of character to stand tall in the face of adversity.

This Bible illustration reminds me of an old saying that goes something like this, "when the going gets tough, the tough get going." Well, just the opposite happened in this moment of truth for these early Christian believers. Instead of standing up and fighting for what they believed in, they decided to walk away. I guess you could say there was too much heat in the kitchen!

However, to be fair, we must account for the actions of the 12 disciples who were the core leaders and part of the inner circle of the Christian movement at the time. In a sense, they were all brothers in Christ, and it was a close-knit family. They were the nucleus of Christ's inner circle. They, too, made decisions during some moments of truth that they wished they had the opportunity to take back (understanding, of course, that God is in control and that His perfect will was to be accomplished).

During the arrest and betrayal of Jesus, His disciples were nowhere to be found. They took off and disassociated themselves from the Lord—an approach that many of us use in our individual moments of truth and in crisis situations if we are being totally honest. Here, we find a gut-wrenching and almost agonizing verse that describes a moment of truth for many of His followers:

"And they all forsook him, and fled" (Mark 14:50).

Just think about this! The Savior of the world was being unjustly accused and arrested, and His core followers and leaders fled! They didn't have the intestinal fortitude, temerity, or faith to stand up and make a difference. The story of Peter's denial especially pulls at the heartstrings of Christian loyalty:

And Peter followed him afar off even into the palace of the high priest: and he sat with the servants, and warmed himself at the fire. (Mark 14:54)

And the second time the cock crew. And Peter called to mind the word that Jesus said unto him. Before that cock crow twice, thou shalt deny me thrice. And when he thought thereon, he wept. (Mark 14:72)

Peter's example is such a powerful story of human weakness, lack of courage, and faithlessness. And while impetuous Peter started out like gangbusters and cut off the ear of a servant of the high priest, his discipline, determination, and faithfulness started to wane during this particular crisis moment.

Each of us should take notice that we, too, could be caught in moments of truth and other decision-making situations that may not honor the Lord. We need to plead and be stretched out before the Lord, asking Him to direct our paths. We must ask Him to enlarge our measure of faith so we can do the right thing and make the best decisions possible.

Fortunately, there is a much better ending for most of the core disciples (Judas being the exception) relating to their Christian faith, leadership, and impact. After a rocky start, the core disciples made lifelong commitments to serve the Lord with all their hearts, minds, and souls. The Bible and history record that most were on fire and zealous for the cause of Christ and were eventually martyred (John's exile to Patmos is the exception).

What is the key takeaway and points of contemplation for Christians today? When at your place of employment and a coworker tells an off-color joke, how do you handle that moment of truth? Yes, there are even those who will knowingly discredit, ridicule, and mock the Christian faith in your very presence. They will blatantly smear and make fun of our Lord and Savior Jesus Christ. How will you respond in that moment of truth? What about when the progressive liberal factions of our society try to limit our worship to the four walls of a church building? Will you rise to the occasion and make the right choices to defend the faith?

In conclusion, as Christian leaders, we should be on the lookout and embrace those defining moments of truth. We should handle those situations with Christlike humility and love. They should be viewed as opportunities to bring praise and adoration to our Lord and Savior Jesus Christ. We should not shy away or follow "afar off" when it is within our power and God-given gifts to do something. How we handle each moment of truth will define our Christian character. They are a collection of vital decision points that tell a lifelong story of who we are as individuals. How will you handle your next moment of truth? What effect will you have on the future?

---

[1] https://dictionary.cambridge.org/dictionary/english/moment-of-truth

23

GROUND LEVEL – PLUS ONE

The internalized knowledge of our Creator moves us with the grace and ease necessary to build enduring trust.

KING DAVID'S POWER AND influence grew mightily during his seven-and-a-half years of independent rule while at Hebron. He became king over all Israel. For the most part, David consolidated forces during this time by using much wisdom, discernment, and political maneuvering. Through conquest, servitude, alliance building, or allegiances pledged to him from those who wanted to be on the right side of history (and stay alive), King David masterfully put together a mandate to wrest full control of power and lead the nation of Israel.

One way he consolidated power and authority was by being an intelligent dispenser of information with a communication style that involved all levels of his organization of governance, along with those citizens at the ground level. David understood the power and symbolic importance of keeping everyone involved and in the loop on major decisions. Well, almost everyone!

His kingly approach of getting down to the ground level is a textbook leadership style that everyone in organizational life can learn from. Keeping close to the masses and allowing them to contribute a voice in crucial matters helps build morale and teamwork, ultimately leading to collaboration, buy-in, and consensus.

Abraham Lincoln called it, "taking public opinion baths." What happens when we leave out the "One" who is most able to impact the course of history?

We read in 1 Chronicles 13:1–4 the following discourse:

> And David consulted with captains of thousands and hundreds, and with every leader. And David said unto all the congregation of Israel, If it seem good unto you, and that it be of the Lord our God, let us send abroad unto our brethren every where, that are left in all the land of Israel, and with them also to the priests and Levites which are in their cities and suburbs, that they may gather themselves unto us: And let us bring again the ark of our God to us: for we inquired not at it in the days of Saul. And all the congregation said they would do so: for the thing was right in the eyes of all the people.

At first glance, I see a leadership style in King David that is full of discernment, wisdom, and right on the money. His style brings King David among the people without fear, soliciting their opinions on a matter of critical spiritual importance (moving the ark). Every good organization and leader should be practicing this style of leadership (getting on the ground level) in some way.

However, what is so paradoxical (and creates the conundrum) about the verses above is the stated intent to more diligently inquire of God when the ark is among them. Unfortunately, they immediately proceed to move the ark of God with only a cursory mention of the Lord.

First Chronicles 13:2 states, "and that it be of the Lord our God." That is like someone about to make a major decision in present day speak, saying, "If it's the Lord's will." It also reminds me of the verse that says, "Be ye warmed and filled." This sounds to me like mere words with little-to-no heartfelt significance and God-honoring inquiry. Nowhere in the rest of the chapter does it even mention going to God in solemn and earnest prayer about the pending decision to move the ark. The results of that decision not to seek the Lord in diligent prayer were disastrous and cost a human life. In 1 Chronicles 13:9–10, we read the following:

> And when they came unto the threshing floor of Chidon, Uzza put forth his hand to hold the ark; for the oxen stumbled. And the anger of the Lord was kindled against Uzza, and he smote him, because he put his hand to the ark: and there he died before God.

If David and the people of Israel had "inquired of God" before moving the ark, would God have reminded them of the holy nature of the ark and the utmost care necessary in its removal based on previous divine instruction? Could they have saved the life of Uzza and given the ark the holy and righteous respect it deserved?

It appears that it may have been more David's desire (and the consenting people of Israel) to move the ark at that particular time than it was the Lord's desire. In this biblical account, we also see much sacrifice, dancing, and fanfare, with no indication of King David earnestly seeking God's face on this matter.

If David had consulted with God, he wouldn't have been displeased and/or surprised at the outcome of Uzza's death. God would have reminded them of His divine plan for carrying the ark. The breach upon Uzza would have been understood by all involved based on God's repeated instruction. While the entire circumstance of relocating the ark was a costly teaching moment based on the sacred nature of the ark of God, it is one that King David took to heart. After a brief temper-tantrum of displeasure, we read in the very next chapter—1 Chronicles 14:8–10—how David handled his next major decision:

> And when the Philistines heard that David was anointed king over Israel, all the Philistines went up

to seek David. And David heard of it, and went out against them. And the Philistines came and spread themselves in the valley of Rephaim. And David inquired of God, saying, Shall I go up against the Philistines? and wilt thou deliver them into mine hand? And the Lord said unto him, Go up; for I will deliver them into thine hand.

Communicating with people at the ground level of the organizations and ministries we are responsible for is of utmost importance. However, most vital is our heartfelt determination to seek the opinion of God (Plus One) when making major decisions. The "Plus One" in the title of this article should be first and foremost in our approach to righteous decision-making. How are you doing with your "Plus One" decisions? Have you allowed room for the Creator God to impact major decisions in your life?

24

SOARING DOWN SNOWBALL MOUNTAIN

Confessing our sins is the easy part, but forsaking them is another matter entirely.

MANY OF US SNOWBIRDS (a.k.a. Northerners) can look back to our formative years with great delight at the emergence of the winter season's first snowfall. The leaves had long since fallen to the ground and withered in preparation for creation's blustery winter encampment along with the big chill effect that lay directly ahead.

Or perhaps you grew up in the South where, on occasion, you were blessed with that rare sighting of those little white puffballs accumulating to the point where the ground was fully covered for a few hours or even several days. With childlike excitement and anticipation, you may have headed outdoors to try your hand at "rolling" your first snowman of the new winter season. You started out with a small baseball-sized snowball and rolled it to the point where it was round and large enough for you to design your own personalized snow creature. The longer and further you rolled, the larger and more imposing of a figure could be created! It was a fun and a safe diversion that helped us usher in the long winter months we were about to experience.

However, in the extreme, those same little snowballs heading down the side of a mountain could be treacherous. We have all witnessed on our television sets or in person the effects of an avalanche roaring down the side of a mountain with enough momentum to wipe out entire towns or portions thereof. Those avalanches started out with little sections of snow getting dislodged, growing into uncontrollable slides of snow and debris. The momentum it creates contains so much force that little is left in its wake. The word "powerful" seems wholly inadequate to describe the awe-inspiring rumble, devastation, and force that comes with such momentum.

Reading through the book of Numbers in my daily devotions, I recognized a similar snowball. No, the Israelites had not found a way to roll the manna from heaven into works of art! Neither did the wilderness provide any opportunity for such play. What they did learn, however, was how to create momentum (down Snowball Mountain) that generated such force that it left a trail of destruction.

We all remember the account of the 12 spies sent to Canaan to search out the land and report back what they had found. Moses and the Israelites were about to enter the promised land (so they thought) and wanted to get a bird's-eye view of the people, the land, fortresses, and what they were up against when conquering the land:

> And the Lord spake unto Moses, saying, Send thou men, that they may search the land of Canaan, which I gave unto the children of Israel: of every tribe of their fathers shall ye send a man, every one a ruler among them. (Num. 13:1–2)

What is also noteworthy is that the men who were sent were the actual leaders of their respective tribe from the 12 tribes of Israel. One might say they were some of the best and brightest leaders of their day to have reached such positions of authority and influence. So off they went to spy out the land and bring back news of what they potentially would encounter when invading and conquering the land of Canaan.

Upon their return, most of the spies brought back reports that were chock-full of unbelief and negativity. Ten of the 12 spies (Joshua and Caleb being the exceptions) had a bad case of the "ya-but" disease — "Ya-but" this, "ya but" that. They had drifted so far off course from their spiritual center and relationship with the Lord, that the momentum they had created with their unbelief was headed down a mountain that would lead to destruction. Their report included the following details:

> Nevertheless the people be strong that dwell in the land, and the cities are walled, and very great: and moreover we saw the children of Anak there. The Amalekites dwell in the land of the south: and the Hittites, and the Jebusites, and the Amorites, dwell in the mountains: and the Canaanites dwell by the sea, and by the coast of Jordan. (Num. 13:28, 29)

The 10 spies were basically saying that they served a small and puny God whom they could not take at His Word. The peoples of the land were too big and strong; there were giants in the land; the fortresses were insurmountable; and they held the lowlands and highlands and would surround them if they initiated an attack.

The spies concluded that God was wrong and that they should not proceed! "Oh, thou of little faith!" We must also remember that the little "snowballs" of momentum of unbelief had started years earlier and their unbelief manifested itself in numerous ways. Let us recap just a few of those momentum-building occurrences that preceded their reports of unbelief.

- Constant complaining and murmuring from the Israelites

- Fleshly desires (lust from the influence of the mixed multitude)
- Discontentment (the manna was not good enough, they wanted flesh)
- Complaint of Moses
- Miriam and Aaron speak against Moses
- Asked for a captain and wanted to return to Egypt
- Korah's rebellion
- Other blatant examples of disrespect and dishonor to God

Yes, the snowball of unbelief and faithlessness was gaining speed and momentum at an accelerating pace. Unfortunately, the incident with the 12 spies was just the latest example in a long line of sinful indiscretions that would continue to "plague" (pun fully intended) the nation until the Lord ultimately stayed His hand. He punished them with several specific examples:

- An abundance of quail and the subsequent plague
- Miriam's leprosy
- Prohibiting the Israelites from entering the promised land
- Death in the wilderness (for those 20 years old and up)
- Death of the 10 spies
- Death of the 250 men who were power hungry and wanted to usurp the authority of Moses and Aaron
- 14,700 who died in an additional plague for their continued murmuring
- Many smote and discomfited by the Canaanites

Have you ever tried to walk back or unroll a snowball? Think about it for a minute. Have you ever tried to reverse the unrelenting and powerful force of a landslide headed down the side of a mountain? It just doesn't work that way in the flesh, and the Israelites faced this dilemma head-on. God told them that because of their unbelief, they would die in the wilderness:

> I the Lord have said, I will surely do it unto all this evil congregation, that are gathered together against me: in this wilderness they shall be consumed, and there they shall die. (Num. 14:35)

Foolishly, when the Israelites realized their sinful ways, they presumed to move forward and attack the inhabitants of the land of Canaan. This went against the very Word of the Lord. They were trying to get out from under their sinful ways with fleshly motives and desires. At this point, they were still not in synch with God Almighty and His perfect will!

Fortunately, there is an important lesson for us to take away that gives us great hope in the Lord when we are headed down Snowball Mountain. When, like Israel, we sin and leave the presence of a holy and righteous God, He has given us the ability to escape. We escape by repenting, asking forgiveness, and resting in our Lord and Savior Jesus Christ! He is our blessed hope for eternity!

Moses stood as a "type" of Christ in this illustration, as we can see in the verse below. If you are a sinner who needs the Lord, won't you trust in Him today? If you are a Christian headed down Snowball Mountain, won't you rest in Him with all your heart, mind, soul, and strength? Praise God in the highest!

> And he stood between the dead and the living; and the plague was stayed. (Num. 16:48)

25

GOD'S TURNAROUND EXPERT

Discernment is the most unnatural, unexplainable, and otherworldly sense of comprehension that helps us level-set the complexities of this present world in light of absolute truth.

THERE ARE TIMES IN the business world when everything seems to be out of synch. The boss is upset, customers are enraged, and the employees are just fed up with the status quo and are headed out the door in droves. There is no passion, focus, or vision for where the organization is headed and what they hope to accomplish in the long-term. These can be very trying times in the business world and organizational life in general for all involved.

Fortunately, trying times call for special and gifted leaders who will step up and lead. They lead in ways that exhibit much determination, inspiration, discernment, and prayer to see the project, business issue, or even the organizational life cycle through to the end. These special leaders have an acute understanding that God has placed them in the exact circumstance to make a difference.

The Bible story that we are going to explore is a model for taking an organization from the depths of despair to one of prominence. Let's consider each of the leadership traits and the strategies employed by King Hezekiah that helped move the nation of Israel back to a God-consciousness. God used King Hezekiah and his gifts to bring glory to Himself. Can the strategies used by

God's turnaround expert in 2 Chronicles help impact your organization?

King Hezekiah understood the absolute travesty that had taken place (and continued to take place) with the nation of Israel. He knew without question that they had forsaken the Lord God Almighty and set their hearts on idols and other pagan distractions. He also understood that the paths on which their forefathers had taken them was leading to utter spiritual and physical destruction. It was a path so vile and full of pagan ritual and apostasy that their very existence hinged on their willingness to "turn" and worship the one true God. The portion of the Bible we will be looking at in this chapter should remind Christians everywhere of our need for repentance, rebirth, and renewal.

Understanding the Root Cause

> For our fathers have trespassed, and done that which was evil in the eyes of the Lord our God, and have forsaken him, and have turned away their faces from the habitation of the Lord, and turned their backs. (2 Chr. 29:6)

Hezekiah knew that Israel was in the eye of a storm and in the grasp of God's mighty wrath and judgment. Something had to be done, and it was going to take a strong, disciplined, and committed leader to stand up and articulate an alternative direction back to the foundations of the faith. Yes, they must immediately "turn" back to the face of the Lord.

> Wherefore the wrath of the Lord was upon Judah and Jerusalem, and he hath delivered them to trouble, to astonishment, and to hissing, as ye see with your eyes. (2 Chr. 29:8)

Taking Ownership and Responsibility

> Now it is in mine heart to make a covenant with the
> Lord God of Israel, that his fierce wrath may turn
> away from us. (2 Chr. 29:10)

Hezekiah's visionary plea and encouragement to Israel carried a direct responsibility of obedience from the nation (corporately) and the people (individually) along with a heavenly expectation that the Spirit of God would be at work and move.

Creating the Vision

> My sons, be not now negligent: for the Lord hath cho-
> sen you to stand before him, to serve him, and that ye
> should minister unto him, and burn incense.
> (2 Chr. 29:11)

What is so refreshing about this portion of Scripture is how the people of Israel saw the error of their ways (repentance); made the necessary spiritual adjustments by turning (rebirth); and then put a plan in place to do something about their wayward behavior (renewal). Furthermore, once God's Spirit started to move, there was an immediacy to their action. It was a force so powerful that it consumed their very thoughts, desires, and actions:

> And they gathered their brethren, and sanctified
> themselves, and came, according to the command-
> ment of the king, by the words of the Lord, to cleanse
> the house of the Lord. (2 Chr. 29:15)

Division of Labor and Accountability

In their focus and delight in charting a new path for the Lord, temple worship was restored, vessels sanctified, sacrifice and offerings reinstituted, and atonement was made for all Israel. Hezekiah even brought back the sacred sound of music with cymbals, psalteries, harps, and trumpets:

> And he set the Levites in the house of the Lord with cymbals, with psalteries, and with harps, according to the commandment of David, and of Gad the king's seer, and Nathan the prophet: for so was the commandment of the Lord by his prophets. (2 Chr. 29:25)

Relying on God

What is especially comforting about the events of this period is the way the Spirit of God worked. The Lord used the strong leadership capabilities of Hezekiah to lead the people to becoming obedient and willing servants. However, we must also notice that a sovereign God moved in the hearts of the people at the same time:

> And Hezekiah rejoiced, and all the people, that God had prepared the people; for the thing was done suddenly. (2 Chr. 29:36)

Revival

> So there was great joy in Jerusalem: for since the time of Solomon the son of David king of Israel there was not the like in Jerusalem. (2 Chr. 30:26)

It should help remind us that when "man moves" through human invention, worldly ingenuity, and in a sin-filled world, our thoughts and our ways are limited and confined. When "man moves," he generally explores the depths and extremities of the usual and mundane. But when "God moves," the energy, passion, and hope we have for a brighter tomorrow is exponentially multiplied by the working of the Holy Spirit.

God uses people for the furtherance of His kingdom. He used Hezekiah to help get the nation of Israel back on track. Will you let God use you as a leader to impact others in your place of business? Will you let Him use you to help revive the hearts of the people in your community, entrepreneurial venture, corporate setting, nonprofit, family, or ministry organization? Praise God for a leader's vision and the corresponding plea from King Hezekiah! Praise God for business leaders who stand up, take charge, and lead! Are you God's next turnaround expert?

26

THE ROAD TO AGREEMENT

Getting along requires self-denial, introspection, and the actions necessary for us to walk in the Spirit as we strive to impact the culture.... but it never includes compromise.

AS FUNDAMENTAL CHRISTIAN BELIEVERS, we must never compromise biblical truths, standards, precepts, and moral absolutes found in God's Word for the sake of expediency— political or otherwise. However, we should be ever-mindful to be peaceful, loving, and gentle souls with a willingness to move toward areas of agreement and common purpose for the good of others, knowing that this will in no way bring a perfect solution in the minds of either party.

Every decision we make toward this endeavor should be for the glory of God, not for the self-aggrandizing rewards and prideful ends of man's evil machinations. In the end, if the basis for dialogue and common ground is either not available or simply impossible based on biblical moral deviation, we then diligently seek those who would agree to fight common enemies that would do harm to the cause of Christ.

As a nation, we must preserve the absolute biblical moral standards contained in the Word of God at all costs. The disintegration of these moral standards in society will create the demise and subsequent exit of our country from a position of authority and greatness to one that places us in the realm of the irrelevant.

27

THE BALANCED WORD OF GOD

The Christ-child grew until the time appointed, when He selflessly fulfilled the final chapter of the old covenant with His blood.

WE MUST BE ACUTELY aware of the extreme and fringe elements that do great harm to the cause of Christ in our churches across America. The enemy has masterfully used those who would propose biblical doctrines and preferences in the extreme. Satan has been extraordinarily successful in tainting sound doctrine with man-made opinions not clearly evident in God's Word.

Many of us feel we could be guilty by association if we go too far in any one direction that seems to support these positions. In the rest of this chapter, we'll look at several points of biblical doctrine where our thinking and worship is being limited/impacted because of the extreme and fringe elements found in our religious institutions.

> All Scripture is given by inspiration of God, and is profitable for doctrine, for reproof, for correction, for instruction in righteousness. (2 Tim. 3:16)

Holy Spirit

I believe that the extremes of emotionalism and the charismatic movement are having a negative impact on the way fundamental

Christians relate to and worship the Holy Spirit. We are so concerned about mimicking those extreme elements because we do not want to be cast as one of them.

Make no mistake—I believe that tongues have ceased in the modern age of Christianity, and human-generated emotionalism has no place in our worship. While I disagree with their extreme positions, I also think that many are brothers and sisters in Christ. This is assuming, of course, that they have repented and trusted in Christ alone for their salvation. However, I disagree with the human-generated "animation" that is often associated with what they call the complete and total filling of the Spirit. I also disagree with any new doctrinal teachings, revelations, and other unusual practices and ordinances not evident in God's Word.

Unfortunately, the effects of disassociation from this extreme and emotional element have left a crater-sized void when worshipping a Creator God in spirit and in truth. God has given us a body, mind, spirit, and soul for the glory of His name. He has also given us emotion with which to worship Him.

The Holy Spirit is on an equal plane with both the Father and the Son. I believe that the Holy Spirit can generate great sensitivity and emotion as we worship the Savior. We need to talk more openly about the Holy Spirit and embrace the Spirit of God on an equal footing. We must not be shy about giving the reverence, glory, and praise to the Spirit's working in our lives. We serve one God in three separate and distinct personages.

> Be glad in the LORD, and rejoice, ye righteous: and shout for joy, all *ye that are* upright in heart. (Ps. 32:11)

> Let everything that hath breath praise the Lord. Praise ye the Lord. (Ps. 150:6)

> For ye shall go out with joy, and be led forth with peace: the mountains and the hills shall break forth

before you into singing, and all the trees of the field
shall clap *their* hands. (Isa. 55:12)

Looking back in history, we can see how Satan has managed
to reframe our thinking on the Holy Spirit. During the "Great
Awakening" period of the early 1700s, God was working miracles
throughout New England, starting with a stirring message (along
with much prayer) from pastor and theologian Jonathan Edwards
from Northampton, Massachusetts. He preached the sermon,
"Sinners in the Hands of an Angry God," which shook people to
their core and led to the realization of their need for a Savior. People were genuinely and authentically crying out to God for redemption and relief from the burden of their sin.

There were guttural utterances from those being convicted
during that time where no one would deny the power of the Spirit
of God. Most of these converts went on to live dedicated Christian
lives for the glory of God. However, Satan could not let this stand.
He had to encroach God's throne and bring the human element to
what started out as a Spirit-led undertaking. There were soon
many irrational, bombastic, and satanic demonstrations in the services that did not originate from our Lord. Men and women began to defraud the Spirit's working with human-generated cries,
screams, and demonstrations that took the focus from His Spirit
and put it squarely on the machinations of man.

Why are we so afraid to embrace the power, joy, and emotion
of God's Spirit? Why do we feel the need to relegate our praise
and worship of our Lord and Savior to an occasional amen? Even
then, we must make sure that we don't shout it too loud and be
pigeonholed as one of them! As Christians, we have the Spirit of
the living God residing inside of us. We must be careful not to
allow Satan to maneuver us into a position where we are not able
to fully express the joy of what it means to serve the great "I AM."

God's Blessings

When Christians earnestly honor, obey, and serve a Risen Savior they should expect to have blessings in this present world and beyond. What is wrong with believing that God will bless you for your obedience? How many "If-Then" scenarios do we see in the Word of God? "If you obey my Word, then you can expect a blessing from above." We do not obey with the motives to receive untold blessings and material riches—we simply obey because God has told us to, and we do so by faith. Our obedience shouldn't spring from a lustful and degenerate heart craving the riches and glory of this present world. No. We obey as an act of selfless worship.

Herein lies another of those extreme examples of how Satan has twisted a foundational truth about obedience and blessing. In the extreme, we have coined what is called the "prosperity gospel." Some would have you believe that financial success and wealth is always the will of God for believers. I disagree. I do not believe that God looks at all Christians in a robotic fashion and suggests that they should have wealth and prosperity. God takes each of us down the paths of life that will mold us into His image. If that path includes financial success and wealth, then so be it. If that path includes being part of middle-America or those who are less fortunate, that is okay too.

Unfortunately, once again we allow the extreme positions of the health and wealth (prosperity) gospel to paint us into a corner where we are afraid to suggest that God is blessing us in a material fashion. How dare we suggest that God is blessing us with wealth (spiritual and material) as we are obedient to Him and His Word? Doesn't that mean God is partial to one group of Christians over another? No, it does not. It simply means that the trials, joys, temptations, and circumstances of life will be varied and different for all of God's children.

No Christian walk is an exact carbon copy. When we are blessed with spiritual and material abundance, we should give

God the honor, praise, and glory due His name. Who else are you going to thank for His abundant provision? We should not be shy about giving God the glory for wealth and riches! It doesn't mean you believe in a "prosperity gospel." It simply means you are giving praise where praise is due!

When I read in the Bible about being blessed and rewarded for my stewardship and obedience, I take it at face value. The error of teaching about health and wealth in Christian circles comes with the motivation and heart condition of the believers in question. If their obedience springs from a pure heart before the Lord and He is blessing them with material abundance, then we should give thanks!

> For of him, and through him, and to him, *are* all things: to whom *be* glory for ever. Amen. (Rom. 11:36)

Fellowship

What a joy it is to fellowship with other Christian believers! The importance of that horizontal covenant bond that helps build one another up in the faith can't be overstated. God uses people to impact the lives of others. He wants us to share in the joys and trials of life and to be helpful to those in need. I think we would all agree that ministering to the needs of church members is a vital function of the local body. We also know that where God's name is being magnified and His Word is being lived out, Satan is in the background trying to destroy everything that is pure, right, and good. Enter in the extremes of a social gospel message.

In this extreme environment, the church body becomes one big playdate. Everything starts to revolve around the social functions of the church and not around the foundational issues of preaching, teaching, and prayer. This extreme works diligently to keep the masses happy and preoccupied with the latest and greatest social event on the calendar. Some would even say that it is party time! In the end, little satisfaction is derived from a social gospel approach. With this approach, the proper alignment between the social, family, spiritual, and workplace are seemingly incongruent and disparate from one another. In reality, we need a balanced approach to fellowship, with proper goals and objectives leading the way.

> Not forsaking the assembling of ourselves together,
> as the manner of some is; but exhorting one another:
> and so much the more, as ye see the day approaching.
> (Heb. 10:25)

God's Grace

If it wasn't for God's grace, mercy, and longsuffering nature, I would be headed for an eternity in hell. There's no other way to put it. His grace is sufficient for all who put their faith and trust in our Lord Jesus Christ. We also know that He is a God of love and that everything that we do here on earth should be done with an eternal view in mind.

We should be mindful of His unmerited favor every moment of every day. Each thought, decision, passion, and action should be taken with the grace of God foremost in our minds. However, what happens when the grace of God is taken to the extreme and there is little room for His righteous judgment, justice, and accountability? Doesn't a grace-only position leave out much of the Bible? Isn't there as much about God's righteous judgment in the Bible as there is about grace, love, and mercy? Why, then, gravitate to a more user-friendly version of God's Word versus the whole counsel of God?

This answer is one of convenience and not wanting to be held accountable to godly standards and forsaking the pleasures of this world. When standards and accountability are introduced, commitment and selflessness must quickly follow. It seems like the world (along with many Christians) wants to take a ride on that

roller coaster of fame, fortune, and fun with little-to-no accountability for their ungodly ways. Christians must never fail to embrace righteous judgment, justice, and accountability in balance
with the grace of God.

> For by grace are ye saved through faith; and that not
> of yourselves: it is the gift of God. (Eph. 2:8)

God's Law

On the opposite end of the spectrum of grace we find those who
cling to a legalistic interpretation of the Bible. With legalism
comes a long list of do's and don'ts discussed in chapter one. In
the extreme, legalists are so concerned with the letter of the law
that they have unknowingly created a works-based form of worship that they would vehemently argue against in the abstract.

However, it is merely a type of ritualistic and formalistic
works-based worship. This form of worship saps the strength and
vitality of the working of the Holy Spirit and brings us to a cold,
judgmental, and lonely place where there is little company. It
doesn't take long for these types of churches to either shrink in
size or disappear altogether.

> Knowing that a man is not justified by the works of
> the law, but by the faith of Jesus Christ, even we have
> believed in Jesus Christ, that we might be justified by
> the faith of Christ, and not by the works of the law:
> for by the works of the law shall no flesh be justified.
> (Gal. 2:16)

God's Sovereign Nature

What a blessing that God, the Creator, in His foreknowledge saw
fit to save me at the beginning of time. The Bible clearly tells us in

Romans that He predestinated us to be conformed to the image of His Son! I take this at face value and believe Him at His Word:

> For whom he did foreknow, he also did predestinate to be conformed to the image of His Son, that he might be the first-born among many brethren. Moreover whom he did predestinate, them he also called: and whom he called, them he also justified: and whom he justified, them he also glorified.
> (Rom. 8:29–30)

On the other hand, man also has a responsibility to call upon the name of the Lord. Man must choose to cry out to be rescued, while freely and willingly accepting that blessed gift of salvation. He has been given a free will to either accept or reject that wonderful hope for tomorrow and turn from his sins. However, the extreme elements in the Hyper-Calvinist tradition would have you believe that there is an elect in God's church and that man's free will would have nothing at all to do with His divine plan. This position fully discredits and disavows much of the teachings of the Bible (see below). In my humble opinion, there is much room to allow for the mystery of God's Word when trying to understand both the Calvinist and Arminian points of view.

> For whosoever shall call upon the name of the Lord shall be saved. (Rom. 10:13)

> So then faith cometh by hearing, and hearing by the Word of God. (Rom. 10:17)

Balance

Yes, what we need all across America is balance, straight from the Word of God. While God Almighty has given us many straightforward principles, promises, commands, and warnings, He also has left a lot of room to maneuver. Unfortunately, man, in turn, takes that maneuverability, freedom, and liberty and twists it into human-forms of Bible doctrine.

We systematize, organize, and intellectualize man's opinion of unclear Scripture to the extreme. Man has built entire denominations and religious sects as a result. We must stay clear of the extreme of man's machinations in areas unknown but embrace the liberty we have in Christ Jesus and the balance found in God's Word. Never allow the extreme positions of man to deter you from seeking the whole counsel of God!

> And Joshua said unto them, Fear not, nor be dismayed, be strong and of good courage: for thus shall the LORD do to all your enemies against whom ye fight. (Josh. 10:25)

28

SEEING GOD IN EVERYDAY LIVING

An innocent pause in the active working of the spiritual mind leads to earthly mush.

A FEW MONTHS BACK, I was sitting at local area restaurant reading my Bible along with a few other books by well-known Christian authors (A. W. Tozer, C.H. Spurgeon, and contemporary Steve Pettit). At the time, I was anticipating a teaching and preaching opportunity with an upcoming trip to India and wanted to adequately prepare by digging into the meat of God's Word. I was sitting there fully contemplating all the things that I read that day, things that were full of wisdom, life, and righteousness!

As I looked around the restaurant, I started to admire a couple of wall hangings and began appreciating the fact that they mentioned our God in heaven above. Then I remembered that I was sitting in the South (South Carolina) and the chances of that happening anywhere else in the world were limited. I then focused my eyes on other parts of the restaurant that were plastered with a bunch of worldly phrases and slogans. One slogan in particular caught my attention: "Because life has forever changed"

I thought about it for a few minutes and then decided to add a few words at the end to give it more of a spiritual connotation, meaning, and application. I changed it to read: "Because life has forever changed through Him and His Spirit."

After reading this a couple of times, I noticed that I could find the word "Christ" in the various letters of the sentence. Well, you probably know what happened next. My mind started to wander, and I made a brief attempt to come up with as many spiritual words as I could possibly find from that one sentence. I challenge you to see how many more words you can come up with!

The lesson of the day is to try finding the beauty of God in everyday living. Be on the lookout for opportunities to give praise and adoration to our Lord and Savior Jesus Christ. Allow this world to become your personal playpen for spiritual blessing. Even a wall at a local restaurant can be used for His glory. Below, are a few words and phrases that can be recreated from the letters in the sentence above. Can you find any more?

God the Father	God's Call
God the Son	Holy
God the Holy Spirit	Spirit
Salvation	Son
Evangelism	Angel
Christ	Son of Man
God	Alpha
Gift	Omega
Run the Race	First
Gave His Son	Last
High Calling	Gift
Glorification	Life
Sanctification	Eternal
Free Gift of Salvation	Trials
Eternal Life	Blessings
Love	Curse
Righteousness	Amen
Blood	Cross
Patience	Freedom

29

OUR PROTECTION FROM ABOVE

Reliance on the Lord is an uncompromising faith, trust, and submission.

WHAT DO THE WORDS shadow, encampeth, hedge, rest, abide, and seek all have in common? They are powerful descriptions and vivid imagery that bring to mind "kept hearts and minds" by "the peace that passeth all understanding through Christ Jesus" (Phil. 4:7). We have this peace because Christ reaches out with His everlasting arms to comfort and protect us. They are the comforts that only born-again believers can experience as they put their faith and trust in Him. This peace brings us to a place of serenity in the newness of life realized. It's a place of untold devotion, faith, and humility before the Creator God. It soothes the hearts, minds, and souls of those who diligently seek that sacred place of love and commitment. Let's now look at how God uses each of these words in the Bible for our comfort and joy.

Shadow – A dark area or shape produced by a body coming between rays of light and a surface.[1]

As David was fleeing the murderous grip of King Saul, he cried out to God for that sweet resting place "in the shadow of thy wings." David's spiritual instincts led him to seek refuge in the only place where he knew he would be safe. David was experiencing calamities in both the physical and spiritual realms. It was a warfare that only God could impact and control.

> Be merciful unto me, O God, be merciful unto me: for my soul trusteth in thee: yea, in the shadow of thy wings will I make my refuge, until these calamities be overpast. (Ps. 57:1)

David knew that the shining power of God's light, and the subsequent shadow it created, would be sufficient as a protective barrier against King Saul's merciless attacks. The radiant hues of light and brightness were (are) in such a state of illumination that all David needed were the shadows cast by God for safety. This was a clear acknowledgement by David of his Lord's awesome power and might. There was no question in David's mind that this was the appropriate resting place and the only place that he could hide.

Encampeth – *To pitch tents or form huts, as an army; to halt on a march, spread tents and remain for a night or for a longer time, as an army or company.*[2]

Is there any better imagery of protection than that of the Lord's angel encamping around Christians who would fear Him? That is exactly what this verse is telling us.

> The angel of the LORD encampeth round about them that fear him, and delivereth them. (Ps. 34:7)

If we truly fear the Lord, He will deliver you from the enemies of this world. This is a promise of elevated and monumental proportions. Fear Him, and the encampment will ensue!

Hedge – *A fence or boundary formed by closely growing bushes or shrubs.*[3]

God's hedge of protection is evident in the life of his devoted servant Job. Satan, himself, acknowledged the protective barrier when he asked God to allow him to "try" Job and his resolve toward the things of the Lord in times of trouble and distress:

> Hast not thou made an hedge about him, and about his house, and about all that he hath on every side? thou hast blessed the work of his hands, and his substance is increased in the land. (Job 1:10)

Basically, Satan was saying that he wanted a "go at" Job without the impenetrable hedge of protection shown to those who are obedient to God. If you recall, Job showed unwavering obedience and devotion to God and was blessed. I believe God also builds a hedge of protection around Christians when we accept Him as Savior. The Holy Spirit and our guardian angels will also "keep us" toward that end.

Rest – *Cease work or movement in order to relax, refresh oneself, or recover strength.*[4]

Not only does God want us to rest in Him so we can refresh ourselves, but He wants us to stop trying to run the race on our own in a frenzied or earthly manner. He wants us to rely on Him and the Spirit of God compared to the weak and depraved intellectual capacity of man trying to direct his affairs in this life. He wants us to practice "skilled living" by resting in His wisdom and might:

> For he that is entered into his rest, he also hath ceased from his own works, as God did from his. (Heb. 4:10)

When we do enter into His rest, God can mightily use man as instruments of His righteous. By contrast, when we fail to enter into His rest, we rely on the power of man versus the power of the Spirit that resides within believers.

Abide – *The power to sustain without flinching or breaking.*[5]

When we abide in Christ, we are acknowledging that the totality of His Word is all that we want or need. We are telling the world that His Word has the power to sustain us for an eternity. In the Bible, whose author is the great "I am", we find the roadmap for the intricacies of life. He is an author so holy and righteous that we must fall prostrate before His throne. Praise the Lord!

There are two verses in John that are especially appropriate and illustrate the point of abiding in Christ:

> Abide in me, and I in you. As the branch cannot bear fruit of itself, except it abide in the vine; no more can ye, except ye abide in me. (John 15:4)

> If ye abide in me, and my words abide in you, ye shall ask what ye will, and it shall be done unto you. (John 15:7)

Seek – *An attempt to find (something).*[6]

What attempt are you making to find the Lord? Are you diligently searching the Scriptures for an understanding of your best friend? God delights in pleasing His children. He wants us to ask, seek, and knock. I pray that we would all seek the riches and wisdom found in His Word. I pray that our seeking and importunity is such that the Lord is fully satisfied with our pleasure

> Ask, and it shall be given you; seek, and ye shall find; knock, and it shall be opened unto you. (Matt. 7:7)

The protective nature of our Lord knows no bounds or limits. God stands ready to accept all those who call upon His name. He stands ready to fortify the encampments and hedges needed for our full and utter protection. Won't you seek Him with all your heart, mind, and soul?

---

[1] https://www.oxforddictionaries.com/

[2] https://av1611.com/kjbp/kjv-dictionary/encamp.html

[3] https://www.oxforddictionaries.com/

[4] https://www.oxforddictionaries.com/

[5] https://anewthingministries.com/the-word-of-god-is/

[6] https://www.oxforddictionaries.com/

30

FUNDAMENTAL VERSUS FOUNDATIONS

Separation is an innate understanding through spiritual discernment that we should not look like, or participate in, the things that the world cherishes.

IN THE WORLD THAT we live in, where perception often becomes reality for many, those not firmly grounded in the Word of God could potentially misunderstand and be confused about fundamental Christianity and what our ultimate vision is for the Lord. While scores of the younger generation continue to support a biblical worldview and understand what true fundamentalism is all about, that simply isn't the case across the board.

In many instances, the enemy has been successful in reframing the Christian belief system among our youth with narratives (storytelling) that deconstruct the fundamental doctrines of our faith. Satan wants us to believe in new iterations of our faith. If he can keep the target moving (biblical truth) with the winds of cultural change, the new iterations will start to look just like the standards of this world. He is working overtime to keep our eyes away from sound teaching and the old-fashioned gospel message. Separation has never been in more danger.

Presently, the world (and many youthful Christians) see fundamentalism as a strict, extreme, and legalistic "process" of living out our faith. They view it as a "process" with a long list of do's and don'ts. The process of living separate and distinct lives through Christian holiness has become repulsive to the world and to many Christians. In many instances, that repulsive orientation toward "righteous process" casts a long shadow over many of our youth in fundamental circles.

Unfortunately, too many of our youth are trying to fit in and cozy up to the standards of the world, with one foot in the world and one foot in Christianity. As a result, that long shadow has had the effect of driving away many of our younger generation. In their eyes, that ridged "process" is much too confining and does not let them express themselves in a way that aligns with their current view of the world and the culture. The need for alignment to our culture among our youth is very troubling. It is an unfortunate scenario, but one that exists just the same. The interconnected nature of our society (technology) has opened the floodgates to worldly spiritual constitutions, contamination, and pleasures.

We must stand ready to lovingly lead our youth away from the cultural manifestations that seek to distort and manipulate the holy and true nature of the Word of God. The culture must never be able to influence, redefine, or exact a form of truth and godly living not found in the Bible.

I believe that the word "foundations" could have an impact over the long-term, assuming the Bible is the guiding light. The older folks will pass away, and I pray that the next generation of leaders in Bible-believing fundamental churches will continue to be focused on the *foundational* biblical precepts, statutes, commandments, laws, and the corresponding principles.

By changing the word *fundamental* to *foundations*, I do not believe we have changed our ultimate focus one bit. The focus for all Christians is, and must always be, giving glory to God. If it does change our focus, then, clearly, we do not have the spiritual roots that are deep enough to overcome the tactics of the world. Over time, I pray that the word "foundations" will come to mean our desire to impact the heart. We want to impact the heart so that

Christians can live holy, separate, and distinct Christian lives. We do this as our hearts draw closer to Him (progressive sanctification) and we are consumed with a *Christian leadership worldview.*

I pray that moving forward, most of the youth in our circles will gain a fuller understanding and appreciation for what true fundamentalism is all about. I also pray that how foundationalism is practiced won't be any different from the way fundamentalism is practiced. In the truest and most sincere way, I am praying that each will constitute an effectual glorification of God Almighty.

In conclusion, I am not so much worried about words and man-made titles. I am most concerned that my family and I will be consistent in reading the Word of God so that we will be changed for His Glory. Let us live the Christ that we see in His Word!

31

SEPARATION OF CHURCH AND STATE

Faith is an intensified spiritual state of mind allowing
one to fully trust that God's will shall prevail even in the
depths of despair and in the severest of afflictions.

OUR CURRENT LAWS THAT support separation of church and state
in the U.S. are simply masquerading as the schoolmaster for religious freedom yet denying the liberty of conscience they were
supposed to protect. These laws were enacted by twisting and
manipulating the contents of a letter written by Thomas Jefferson,
in 1801, from their original intent under the guise of protecting
religious liberty and the free exercise thereof.

Furthermore, while the laws on the books of the United
States Congress might signify a different perspective, rest assured
that separation of church and state has at no time in our country's
history been enforced in total. For the most part, the enforcement
has been specific and limited to the peculiars of the Christian
faith. It has been used to control and stifle Christian freedom and
religious expression.

In this chapter, we are going to look at six defining aspects
of separation of church and state. These will include the First
Amendment, the Danbury Baptist Association letter, Jefferson's

response to that letter, Jefferson's other documented correspondence and beliefs on this issue, the spiritual ramifications, and the
subsequent litigation and court rulings that include Secular Humanism being legally recognized as a religion. While the waters
may be muddied in today's political realm and climate, let us now
look at the purity and simplicity of the first and cherished proclamation in our Bill of Rights.

First Amendment

The first amendment to the constitution is clear. We are not to
make laws that respect a specific religion, and we are not to prohibit the free exercise of one's religion. Pretty simple, huh? How
then have we migrated to such extreme views on this issue? Nowhere in our constitution does it say that the government and/or
its officials can't speak about, express their opinions on, or participate in spiritually motivated activities or events. Nowhere in our
constitution does it say that we should not be able to pray in our
public schools.

The legal folly and anti-God precedence being laid is strategic
and secular in nature. The anti-God and Secular Humanist factions in our society simply do not want the tenants of the Christian faith to be propagated. There are also well-intentioned people
in our country on both sides of the issue who use the term separation of church by indicating that it is written in the constitution.
That is simply not true.

The First Amendment (Amendment I) to the United States
Constitution prevents the government from making laws which
respect an establishment of religion, prohibit the free exercise of
religion, or abridge the freedom of speech, the freedom of the
press, the right to peaceably assemble, or the right to petition the
government for redress of grievances. It was adopted on Decem-
ber 15, 1791, as one of the 10 amendments that constitute the Bill
of Rights.[1]

If the first amendment itself does not address currently defined laws on separation, where did they derive their origin, justification, and so-called legal standing?

The Letter

(From which most of our laws on separation are derived in all their manipulated and derivative forms)

The Danbury Baptist Association of Danbury, Connecticut sent a letter, dated October 7, 1801, to the newly elected President Thomas Jefferson, expressing concern over the lack in their state constitution of explicit protection of religious liberty, and against a government establishment of religion. The letter further cautions Jefferson on the construction of the current Connecticut constitution in that they were being given religious privileges that were in no way considered inalienable.

They feared that without specific language in their constitution relating to religious liberty and the freedom to exercise one's faith, that the next tyrannical leader who assumed executive leadership in Connecticut might withdraw those currently held privileges. Extending religious privileges can quickly be withdrawn in the future while enacting constitutional provisions of religious protection cannot. The Danbury Baptist Association didn't want any privileges or favors from their fellow constituents and/or government officials—they wanted irrevocable and inalienable rights. While they understood that Jefferson had no legal authority to legislate this vital issue in the state of Connecticut, the hope was that his sentiments on religious liberty would be universally shared among all the states. In the letter below, the context of the discussion is clear and concise relating to its main and original premise.

The Address of the Danbury Baptist Association in the State of Connecticut, Assembled October 7, 1801.

To Thomas Jefferson, Esq., President of the United States of America

Sir, Among the many millions in America and Europe who rejoice in your election to office, we embrace the first opportunity which we have enjoyed in our collective capacity, since your inauguration, to express our great satisfaction in your appointment to the Chief Magistracy in the United States. And though the mode of expression may be less courtly and pompous than what many others clothe their addresses with, we beg you, sir, to believe, that none is more sincere.

Our sentiments are uniformly on the side of religious liberty: that Religion is at all times and places a matter between God and individuals, that no man ought to suffer in name, person, or effects on account of his religious opinions, [and] that the legitimate power of civil government extends no further than to punish the man who works ill to his neighbor. **But sir, our constitution of government is not specific.**

Our ancient charter, together with the laws made coincident therewith, were adapted as the basis of our government at the time of our revolution. And such has been our laws and usages, and such still are, [so] *that Religion is considered as the first object of Legislation, and therefore what religious privileges we enjoy (as a minor part of the State)* **we enjoy as favors granted, and not as inalienable rights.** And these favors we receive at the expense of such degrading acknowledgments, as are inconsistent with the rights of freemen. It is not to be wondered at therefore, if those who seek after power and gain, under the pretense of government and Religion, should reproach their fellow men, [or] should reproach their Chief Magistrate, as an enemy of religion, law, and good order, because he will not, dares not, assume the prerogative of Jehovah and make laws to govern the Kingdom of Christ.

Sir, we are sensible that the President of the United States is not the National Legislator and also sensible that the national government cannot destroy the laws of each State, but our hopes are strong that the sentiment of our beloved President, which have had such genial effect already, like the radiant beams of the sun, will shine and prevail through all these States—and all the world—until hierarchy and tyranny be destroyed from the earth. Sir, when we reflect on your past services, and see a glow of philanthropy and goodwill shining forth in a course of more than thirty years, we have reason to believe that America's God has raised you up to fill the Chair of State out of that goodwill which he bears to the millions which you preside over. May God strengthen you for the arduous task which providence and the voice of the people have called you—to sustain and support you and your Administration against all the predetermined opposition of those who wish to rise to wealth and importance on the poverty and subjection of the people.

And may the Lord preserve you safe from every evil and bring you at last to his Heavenly Kingdom through Jesus Christ our Glorious Mediator.

Signed in behalf of the Association, Neh,h Dodge, Eph'm Robbins, The Committee, Stephen S. Nelson[2]

Jefferson's Response

Jefferson's response to the aforementioned letter now echoes in the corridors of religious debate.

> Believing with you that religion is a matter which lies solely between Man & his God, that he owes account to none other for his faith or his worship, that the legitimate powers of government reach actions only, & not opinions, I contemplate with sovereign reverence that act of the whole American people which declared that their legislature should *"make no law respecting an establishment of religion, or prohibiting the free exercise thereof", thus building a wall of separation between Church & State.*[3]

The wall of separation that Jefferson documented and pointed to in the response above was specifically referring to no law respecting an establishment of religion or prohibiting the free exercise thereof. How then did President Jefferson's language get so distorted that, in the 21st century government, officials are prohibited from expressing their religious convictions, and if they do express their beliefs, it is potentially considered a "hate crime" and against the law?

Most in the public sector would be fired on the spot for advocating a religion position. What blasphemy! What utter manipulation to achieve a secular humanist worldview void of any "religious dogma" (their words) by lifting remarks from a friendly and hopeful correspondence between the President and some of his supporting Connecticut constituents.

Unfortunately, what people fail to remember is that Thomas Jefferson put his stake in the ground on religious freedom for those in a civil capacity more than 15 years prior, in the state of Virginia. Nowhere did he narrow his definition of "civil capacity" either to include or exclude specific cultural manifestations (political domain) of those same capacities.

Jefferson's Beliefs

Virginia Statute for Religious Freedom

> Be it enacted by General Assembly that no man shall be compelled to frequent or support any religious worship, place, or ministry whatsoever, nor shall be enforced, restrained, molested, or burthened in his body or goods, nor shall otherwise suffer on account of his religious opinions or belief, but that all men shall be free to profess, **and by argument to maintain, their opinions in matters of Religion, and that the same shall in no wise diminish, enlarge, or affect their civil capacities**. And though we well know that this Assembly elected by the people for the ordinary purposes of Legislation only, have no power to restrain the acts of succeeding Assemblies constituted with powers equal to our own, and that therefore to declare this act irrevocable would be of no effect in law; yet we are free to declare, and do declare that the rights hereby asserted, are of the natural rights of mankind, and that if any act shall be hereafter passed to repeal the present or to narrow its operation, such act will be an infringement of natural right. (Originally authored by Jefferson and championed by Madison, guaranteeing that no one may be compelled to finance any religion or denomination. Statute enacted into law in 1786)[4]

My argument is that Jefferson included civil government as part of those civil capacities. His thoughts in written correspondence as well as his actions support a holistic understanding of inclusion relating to our religious freedoms and activities. Even as President of the United States, he attended worship services in public buildings (see below) belonging to the Federal government.

Jefferson therefore attended (John) Leland's service and then proceeded to attend services regularly in the House (and to permit other federal buildings to be used for services). If that was Jefferson's intent, he seems to have succeeded, but Hutson nevertheless defends Jefferson against charges of hypocrisy, noting that Jefferson had attended worship services in public buildings before becoming President, both in Washington and in Virginia.[5]

If Jefferson's actions and the totality of his thinking on this issue did not in any way constrain one's religious demonstration of their faith, what is the root of all the fussing and squabbling on separation of church and state?

Spiritual Ramifications

Beyond the legal maneuvering and parsing of intent and words through voluminous court proceedings, what are the spiritual forces that we are contending with relating to separation of church and state? The fight is for the means to influence, persuade, and condition our earthly spiritual understanding toward an appointed eternality of existence and being. The fight is between good and evil. The fight is of a spiritual nature. The fight is between the proponents of darkness and those that rest in the light of God's glory.

> For we wrestle not against flesh and blood, but against principalities, against powers, against the rulers of the darkness of this world, against spiritual wickedness in high places. (Eph. 6:12)

There are two forces concurrently at work in the politics and policies of our democratic republic. First, the redeemed (true Christian believers) knowingly allow their Christianity and associated biblical worldviews to inform their political views and policy-making. All mature believers want every aspect of their political policy-making identity to be aligned with God's Word. The way that they think, act, legislate, and deliberate in the body politic should reflect the holy and righteous nature of God. Second, the world (non-Christians) either knowingly or unknowingly allows their personal humanist philosophies and worldviews to inform their politics and policies. Government officials who don't have a personal relationship with Jesus Christ are making policy decisions in the flesh that are informed by their human philosophies on life (Secular Humanism), which the Supreme Court, on several occasions, has ruled to be an organized religion.

Subsequent Litigation

There is an abundance of case law and legal rabbit trails that we could take to elaborate on where we are as a country relating to separation of church and state. For the purposes of the remaining part of this chapter, we are going to look at three specific highlights that seem to stir the pot of passion and are essential contributors to our current interpretations and legal precedence on religious liberty. The first is Everson vs. the Board of Education.

Everson v. Board of Education

Everson v. Board of Education, 330 U.S. 1 (1947),[1] was a landmark decision of the United States Supreme Court which applied the Establishment Clause in the country's Bill of Rights to State law. Prior to this decision, the First Amendment's words, "Congress shall make no law respecting an establishment of religion" imposed limits only on the federal government, while many states continued to grant certain religious denominations legislative or effective privileges. This was the first Supreme Court case incorporating the Establishment Clause of the First Amendment as binding upon the states through the Due Process Clause of the Fourteenth Amendment. The decision in Everson marked a turning point in the interpretation and application of disestablishment law in the modern era.

The case was brought by a New Jersey taxpayer against a tax-funded school district that provided reimbursement to parents of both public and private schooled people taking the public transportation system to school. The taxpayer contended reimbursement given for children attending private religious schools violated the constitutional prohibition against state support of religion, and the use of taxpayer funds to do so violated the Due Process Clause. The Justices were split over the question of whether the New Jersey policy constituted support of religion, with the majority concluding these reimbursements were "separate and so indisputably marked off from the religious function" that they did not violate the constitution.

Both affirming and dissenting Justices, however, were decisive that the Constitution required a sharp separation between government and religion and their strongly worded opinions paved the way to a series of later court decisions that taken together brought about profound changes in legislation, public education, and other policies involving matters of religion. Both Justice Hugo Black's majority opinion and Justice Wiley Rutledge's dissent defined the First Amendment religious clause in terms of a "wall of separation between church and state."[6]

The two key takeaways in this first highlight are that the Establishment Clause is now binding upon States and both majority and dissenting opinions referenced the terminology "wall of separation between church and state." Justices Black and Rutledge's reference had no legal authority and were well out of bounds (and context) when utilizing comments from the President's response to the Danbury Baptist Association. As a result, it had the impact of tightening the noose around the necks of our religious freedoms.

The phrase "secular humanism" became prominent after it was used in the United States Supreme Court case Torcaso v. Watkins. In the 1961 decision, Justice Hugo Black commented in a footnote, "Among religions in this country which do not teach what would generally be considered a belief in the existence of God are Buddhism, Taoism, Ethical Culture, **Secular Humanism,** and others."

Secular Humanism

Secular Humanism is a religion "for Free Exercise Clause purposes." The Court has undeniably defined Secular Humanism as a religion "for free exercise purposes." When Secular Humanists want the benefits of a religion, they get them.

> **Tax Exemption**. Secular Humanism has been granted tax-exempt status as a religion. The Torcaso quote cited the cases.
>
> **Conscientious Objection**. Even though Congress originally granted conscientious objector status only to those who objected to war for religious reasons (i.e., because of a belief in God), the Supreme Court turned around and said that Humanists who don't believe in God are "religious" for C.O. purposes. U.S. v. Seeger, 380 U.S. 163, 183, 85 S.Ct. 850, 13 L.Ed.2d 733, 746 (Holding that belief in a "Supreme Being" is not a necessary component of "religion," quoting a Secular Humanist source, "Thus the 'God' that we love . . . is . . . humanity.")

So Secular Humanism is emphatically and undeniably a religion—"for free exercise purposes."

Any claim that "the clear weight of the case law" is against the proposition that Secular Humanism is a religion is a misleading claim. Secular Humanism is a religion "for free exercise clause purposes."

Secular Humanism is Not a religion "for Establishment Clause purposes."

But when Christians attempt to get the religion of Secular Humanism out of the government schools, based on the same emotional frame of mind which atheists had when they went to court against God in schools, then pro-secularist courts speak out of the other side of their faces and say that Secular Humanism is NOT a religion "for establishment clause purposes." This is slimy, deceitful legalism at its worst.

But it explains why so many are confused about whether Secular Humanism is a religion.

Here is the rule: When Secular Humanists want the benefits of religion, Secular Humanism is a religion. When Secular Humanists are challenged for propagating their religion in public schools, it is not a religion. If that sounds insane, it is; but all insane people are still rational. This insanity is cloaked in the rational-sounding rhetoric of constitutional law. Remember:

Secular Humanism is a religion "for free exercise clause purposes," and it is not a religion "for establishment clause purposes."[7]

Released Time Program

Released Time Program – Zorach v. Clauson, 343 U.S. 306 (1952), was a case in **which the Supreme Court of the United States considered a school district allowing students to leave school for part of the day to receive religious instruction**. This was considered a big win for all religions when the Supreme Court ruled that released time did not violate the Establishment Clause.[8]

So, the questions must be asked. If the tenants of man-made philosophies and the rudiments of secular thinking further propagate and support the Secular Humanist religion, why are they allowed into the public domain (government circles and public schools) if we truly have a separation of church and state? Why would they get a pass and preferential treatment over that of other religions? Why would they be allowed to indoctrinate their public policies and our children with "worldly" beliefs that spew anti-God rhetoric, tearing down the very fabric of Christian beliefs and that of other religions?

If Humanists have been given the legal privileges to be able to condition the minds of their constituents and our young people toward the doctrines of humanity, why not us? If we are going to be totally transparent with the answers to these questions, we must conclude that people in our culture believe one or more of the following:

- They don't believe that what they are teaching or the policies they are creating have a religious intent
- They don't understand the spiritual nature of what is taking place in the public domain
- They haven't connected the dots to the strategy and tactics being used by humanists in the public domain or don't care
- They fully understand that what they are teaching and the policies they are creating support a humanist agenda
- They fully understand that it is a spiritual battle in nature
- They are aware that what they do is strategic in nature accompanied with tactics used to support specific humanist causes

Whether through ignorance, misunderstanding, naivety, or with intent, the teaching and/or policies of humanist thinking leave a long hard trail of anti-God sentiment and vitriol. The Christians, as well as voices of other religions, are being shut out and confined to the four walls of a church building while Secular Humanists have been given the key to the cities and towns of our great country. Ladies and gentlemen, *that* is the great sham of separation of church and state.

---

[1] https://en.wikipedia.org/wiki/First_Amendment_to_the_ United_States_Constitution

[2] https://en.wikisource.org/wiki/Letter_to_the_Danbury_Baptists_- _January_1,_1802

[3] https://en.wikisource.org/wiki/Letter_to_the_Danbury_Baptists_- _January_1,_1802

[4] https://en.wikipedia.org/wiki/Virginia_Statute_for_Religious_Freedom

[5] https://en.wikipedia.org/wiki/Separation_of_church_and_state_in_ the_United_States

[6] https://en.wikipedia.org/wiki/Everson_v._Board_of_Education

[7] web.archive.org/web/20130521123706/http://vftonline.org/Patriarchy/ definitions/humanism_religion.htm

[8] https://en.wikipedia.org/wiki/Zorach_v._Clauson

32

THINKING THROUGH THE ISSUES

The weak will find a convenient way to rationalize their acceptance of the world's "new normal" while marginalizing those who don't.

Activism

- The bright light of a shooting star is a magnificent display of brilliance, tantalizing the senses for an instant
- The constant companionship of the North Star gives us the necessary luminescence and vision to guide us on our way......steady as she goes

Ambassadors

- Spiritually enlightened diplomats serving God on earth for a short period of time
- Those faithful servants willing to be doers of His Word

Atonement

- The selfless act of reconciliation
- A loving sacrifice

Automobiles

- The most exasperating and diminishing asset known to man
- Buy used, get handy, learn patience

Awakened

- The exact opposite of "woke"
- An illumination of body, mind, and soul through the wisdom provided by the Spirit of God without deference to human reasoning and cultural understanding

Baptism

- A born-again believer who wants to publicly identify with the death, burial, and resurrection of our Lord Jesus Christ
- A testimony for the ages acknowledging that one has accepted that free gift of salvation and believes
- The most important declaration of one's inner spiritual convictions to the world

Bible Reading

- The idiosyncratic nature of one's dark side should be crushed at first dawn

- The power and influence of His Word must be switched to the "on position" as the REM of sweet and peaceful rest gives way to the echoes of His creation

Busybodies

- The idle tales and chaff of a few do much to destroy the reputations of the upright
- One who is best suited to play in the sandbox of one's own life, leaving the design of others to their specific approbation

Children

- This is a God-honoring responsibility
- Raising children in the nurture and admonition of the Lord is one of the highest spiritual callings and vocations known to man
- My wife is the better half

Church

- The paradoxical dwelling place of a bunch of righteous misfits perfectly formed, reeling from the impediments of an old sin nature, while basking in the blessed work and hope of the cross
- There is no such community of kindred souls and likeminded brethren as when one desires to step forth into the holiest of holies following the call of a righteous Savior and becoming citizens of His body of believers

Clothing

- This is a necessary evil
- Dress sharp and look good when it's time—or when your spouse says so

Commentary

- This is a second-rate work of another's perfect design. It helps us get an additional perspective, but please be careful with over use
- We get our heads full of other men's opinions and preach those opinions like they are the oracles of God himself
- It is an alternative to studying the Bible and the original language and letting the Spirit of God move you to proclaim what He has shown you through His Word

Confession

- Confessing our sins is the easy part
- Forsaking them is another matter entirely

Constitution of the United States

- When a most sincere and righteous framework has stood the test of time, one can only conclude that it was directed by the hand of God
- The best that men could offer in the culture of that time; giving us the wiggle room to right the ships of necessity; while staying the course to the traditional and original intent and understanding of its unifying accord

Correction

- The chastening of the Lord is hard, redirecting the impurities of mind and soul to the glories of a redeeming God
- Telling me stirs me to expand my thinking; showing me allows me to see the demonstration of an experience; chastening me allows me to grow in the wisdom of the Lord through participation

Debate

- The conditions in which civilized society can passionately express their opinions in the most collegial terms available
- Taking one's convictions out for a spin in the realm of public opinion fully understanding that his/her words have meaning and impact

Debt

- This is servitude in its most ugly and wretched form
- The servants of debt are imprisoned and limited in their spiritual range of magnitude

Declaration of Independence

- This is a story written to inform mankind down through the ages about how men ought to act, behave, and believe when constituting and directing a free and independent government

- It is a heartfelt statement of choice binding the hearts of countrymen and countrywomen behind the idea and experiment, called America

Discernment

- This is the powerful, spiritual radar of intuition that God equips us with for His glory
- The most unnatural, unexplainable, and other-worldly sense of comprehension that helps us level-set the complexities of this present world in light of absolute truth

Dispensationalism

- This is a lofty and intellectual word created by man that does nothing to help me grow
- It attempts to carve God up into different spiritual dispositions
- Read the entire Bible and let God speak to you — that's all

Dominionship

- It is the responsibility of those who are commissioned to exercise control over the essence of God's creation
- It is God giving the "called" the ultimate authority of control

Economics

- Centralized economies are inefficient and inferior to market economies in the same way dictatorship is inferior to a democratic republic
- Liberties, freedoms, and choices are greatly curtailed in the realms of concentrated power

Education

- Repetition is the vital organ in the body of learning
- An innocent pause in the active working of the spiritual mind leads to earthly mush

Encouragement

- This is an uplifting angelic touch from a person full of grace and wisdom
- It is a soothing word to a downcast soul

Encroachment

- This is something that we do when we try to replace God's will with our own
- We tell God that His plan is not quite right

Entanglements

- This is spiritual resistance in high places
- It represents the noise and machinations of this world

Faith

- Faith is an intensified spiritual state of mind allowing one to fully trust that God's will shall prevail even in the depths of despair and in the severest of afflictions
- Faith becomes increasingly manifest in our daily walk as we travel through the long and arduous tunnel of life seeing periods of both extreme darkness and vibrancy of light, never losing sight of the one true focal point—the lighthouse of Jesus Christ our Lord

Fasting

- The fading use and manifestation of sacrifice that denies the mortal being his fleshly ritual, expectation, and sustenance
- Redirecting soul, spirit, and cause through self-denial

Fear

- When faithless creatures anticipate the next bad thing
- As the planned controls of one's life give way to the alternative manifestation of a functional spiritual reality, pushing mankind to cower in the corner at its loss

Free Will

- The freedom and liberty we have to choose, accept, or reject a predetermined path of experience (earthly realm) and eternality (heavenly realm)
- The highest form of praise or the lowest conditions of humanity

Frugality

- Rely on Him; recalibrate your needs; reorient your wants; buy it used; make it yourself; be content; use it up; make it do; wear it out; do without; pray
- The spiritual discernment in knowing that it takes little of this world's goods to sustain us physically, while it takes none of this world's goods to sustain us spiritually

Giving

- The husband reminds his wife before church to make sure she pays the tithe and puts it in the church offering
- Oh, the wretched and debilitating effects of routine, obligation, and tradition; Lord, the sacrifice I place at your feet I do so with joy and praise

Glorification

- Our heavenly physical and spiritual states before God
- The finality of a race well run

Government

- Command and control give way to the excesses of tyrannical jurisdiction, as each command and each control chips away at the foundation of liberty and freedom itself
- Liberty of conscience demands a system of government where man is not imprisoned by the dictates of a few—let freedom ring!
- An organization of protection from itself, others, and ourselves

Hospitality

- A sacred responsibility to attend to the needs of others as well as Christ unawares
- Love thy neighbor!
- It is the selfless act of letting others view and participate in one of the most important and guarded social circles of all—our family

Humanism

- Represents the 4 C's of apostasy (*contrary* to God's Word; *counterfeit* to absolute truth; **concealing** to those lacking spiritual discernment; and **cancerous** to the soul)
- Feeds the flesh

Judgment

- Judgment is left to the sole discretion of a holy and righteous God

- Reproof, rebuke, and godly chastisement (love) is within the purview of Christian responsibility as we engage in spiritual warfare, remembering to be clean before God and making sure that the motes within have been surgically removed and repaired
- We must understand the difference between the two and articulate a clear position when the world flippantly uses the phrase "we shouldn't judge others" as they attempt to cast dispersion on believers with an incorrect supposition

Justification

- The legal standing before God based on our reconciled nature
- God condescending to the ranks of humanity and suffering so that we can be declared guiltless before our maker

Kingdom

- The lifeblood of God's kingdom is in "the going" contained in the phrase "Go ye therefore" inherent in the Great Commission
- The resulting multiplication and growth of His church allows us to redeem the times and stem the tide of moral apostasy; a task impossible if we forget "the going" by standing fast on a course of shrinking ourselves to spiritual greatness with the idle chatter of Pharisaical bemoaning, postulation, and inaction

Leadership

- "Bust down the doors and take no prisoners," cries the self-proclaimed leader of men
- The Christian leader unassumingly asks, "How can I serve to the glory of God?"

Legal System

- The porous nature of our legal system will lead to the decline of Western Civilization as we know it
- The U.S. must pursue rigorous prosecution of the laws of the land. If there are unjust, antiquated, or misdirected laws in our country, then advocating for their removal and/or reconstitution must be pressed within the confines of civil obedience

Life

- The existence of God in us
- The demonstration of God through us
- The love of God to us

Love

- The bridge that spans the great divide between eternal death and everlasting hope
- An authentic expression of commitment that through perseverance clears a holy and righteous path of communion to the heavenlies

Marriage

- Holy matrimony between a man and a woman
- The symbolic relationship between Christ and His church

Materialism

- The want of gathering pacifies the baser instinct of self-acclamation, self-approbation, self-aggrandizement, and self-promotion, all the while leading to the abyss of self-indulgence
- Contentment, however, harmoniously lives in the present, taking life as it comes with the peace that passeth all understanding, to the glory of God

Missions

- The romanticism of "the going" stirs the embers of our human emotions
- The reality of the service awakens us to the average and ordinary blessings of life hidden in the recesses of daily living

Nature

- The indescribable handiwork of the one true creative genius—God Almighty
- An awe-inspiring spoken display of God's gift to mankind
- The manifestation of the death, burial, and resurrection of Christ hidden in plain sight through His creative design

Neighbors

- Loving our neighbors as ourselves seems like an ideal that cannot be reached and a summit that refuses to be scaled
- Human love focuses on the occurrences of life in the moment, fleetingly impacting the senses
- God's love abounds in all things for those who walk by faith and not by sight

Networking

- In the world's eyes, networking is a means to an end...... It is a superficial process of incrementally gaining something from another to the benefit of oneself with a consumer-like mindset
- On the other hand, fellowship is the sweet correspondence between brethren, looking to give rather than to receive, with an investor like mindset
- Intrinsic motivation is key in this regard

Obedience

- When one believes in, follows, and imitates the attributes of Jesus Christ
- Do right until the cows come home, and then keep on doing right
- Live, breath, and do His Word in an all-consuming manner

Patience

- We long for a quiet and peaceable life through the strength of a forbearing hand

- Lord, when you send the trials of affliction for the patience I need, please be gentle. Don't send too much too fast. Keep me from tragedy, conflict, anxiety, poverty, and affliction, but please, Lord, hurry up and give me patience

Persecution

- The faithful will endure all attempts of the world to stifle the sacred voices of godly reason and commitment—the Christian way of life
- The weak will find a convenient way to rationalize their acceptance of the world's "new normal" while marginalizing those who don't

Politics

- The serious man with guns a-blazing sets a course to change the world
- The spiritual man with discerning eyes desires to influence just one poor soul, leading to contagion

Power

- God's Shekinah Glory
- Falling at the feet of God Almighty as spiritual and everlasting servants

Prayer

- The anointed privilege of gaining access to and coming before an Almighty God with our partitions, requests, supplications, and praise

- It is the knowledge that Christians can talk to, commune with, take refuge in, and sit at the feet of the Great "I Am"

Preaching/Pastoring

- The desire of a most honorable gift and calling
- The watch care over the flock of God comes with enormous responsibility and accountability

Predestination

- God chose Christians.
- The other perfect half of the wholly symmetrical spiritual bond between man's free will and God's sovereign control
- The necessary compliment and comfort when trying to articulate the great chasm surrounding the Armenian and Calvinist worldview paradox

Preparation

- Considering things "well" with the forethought and insight needed
- A fair advantage to the well-advised mind

Prophecy

- Fearless proclamation of absolute truth
- Those who have been given the gift of wisdom to understand the present, while heralding the necessities of things to come

Reliance

- An uncompromising faith, trust, and submission
- A confidence that our cares, wants, needs, and cries will be heard when we cast them at the feet of Christ

Repentance

- When the Spirit of God melts our hearts, crushes our conscience, humbles our souls, and redirects our longings for better spiritual ends
- Divine turning and radical change

Reverence

- The complete and utter 360 degree understanding of who we are in light of the Creator of the universe
- An awe-inspirited state of mind and worship that leads us to the most elevated comprehension of His might and wonder

Salvation

- The Christ-child grew until the time appointed, when He selflessly fulfilled the final chapter of the old covenant with His blood
- With the flair of the ultimate and supreme author, He ushered in a more perfect way in the new covenant written with the grace, hope, and love necessary to fulfill and complete its objective

- Jesus Christ shed His blood for the sins of the world so that all who will trust Him and come to a saving and personal knowledge of Him may spend an eternity in heaven above

Sanctification

- The progressive process of cleansing
- Laying aside the lust of the eyes, the lust of the flesh, and the pride of life for spiritual maturation

Separation

- An innate understanding through spiritual discernment that we should not look like or participate in the things that the world cherishes
- We are set apart for holy and righteous means, never gravitating toward anything that would resemble an unholy alliance with sin and iniquity
- If it looks like, and acts like a duck, it is more than likely at a duck

Separation of Church and State

- While the laws on the books might signify a different perspective, rest assured that separation of church and state has at no time in our country's history been enforced
- Government officials who don't have a personal relationship with Jesus Christ and who are informed by their secular humanist philosophies on life are making policy decisions in the flesh... The Supreme Court has ruled on several occasions that Secular Humanism is an organized religion

- An abridged version of the true intent of an author

Sin

- An unholy alliance to the baser instincts of mankind
- It is the wicked and evil oppression that consumes body, mind, and soul when we yield to its despicable temptations
- The Bible tells us not to set any wicked thing before our eyes
- How are you doing? Seriously, how are you doing?

Singing

- The solemn expressions of joy and praise are best communicated with the rapturous chorus of sweet melody wafting upward with a symphonic burst into the ears of a patient and well-pleased God
- The confessions of almighty power through song are best enjoyed in the quietness of the early morning hours

Stewardship

- A position of leadership to actively direct the affairs of this life by distinguishing oneself as faithful
- Preparation, conditioning, and the refining fire of progressive sanctification through godly persuasion

Teacher

- The most blessed of guiding spiritual confidants
- The most miraculous and uncommon concern for another's future well-being
- A holy calling

Traditionalism

- A closely held way of life that cherishes the simplicity of our interactions, relationships, and the way that we imitate and worship Christ
- The realization that the further we move away from the time of Christ, the more deplorable, self-centered, and anti-God society becomes, negating our will to conform

Trials

- The divine quadrants of the forces used to help us grow spiritually
- God's trials, Satan's temptations, cultural trials, familial relationships, and the trials of the mind are five areas that our Sovereign Lord uses to get us battle-tested and ready for this world and the one beyond
- The severity and uniqueness of those trials are purposefully designed toward our bent

Trust

- Leaders lead. Followers follow. The glue that binds the compatibility of soul and spirit to the required ends is the unwavering ingredients of trust

- The internalized knowledge of our Creator moves us with the grace and ease necessary to build enduring trust

Wealth

- Not interested
- Allow me the ordinary means to provide for my family with neither too much nor too little
- Have the determination to live well below your means, and your ability to serve God in the capacity He desires will increase proportionately

Welfare

- The philanthropic commands and precepts ordained of God and written in His Word should ALWAYS take precedence over legislated entitlements
- Misguided actions over the concern for others have unintended consequences that work in reverse

Wisdom

- We have been given the secret keys to unlock the true meaning of the fear of the Lord and find the knowledge of God
- Let's get busy devouring His Word to the point of exhaustion

Witnessing

- With a bold, selfless, and uncompromising determination, we eagerly set our face like flint to proclaim and communicate the good news of Jesus Christ our Lord
- When the God of this universe willingly condescended to such a low degree by using mankind to communicate and herald the spiritual wonders of His enduring kingdom—Jesus Himself—it left us in a state beyond all intellectual comprehension

Worldliness

- Human beings walking out their earthly existence with a high-minded, prideful, and man-centered understanding of Creation
- These worldly creatures are the ones that have internalized the best that man (humanism) has to offer, enjoying the season, persuading others, and wanting more

Worldview

- It is the heavenly standard used when making earthly decisions
- The filter from which you block the impurities of life and make sense of it all

United States

- A defined geographical barrier of protection for the freedoms and liberties of conscience that a sovereign God has ordained and so richly blessed us with that I am pleased to call my country
- A hiding place and a refuge for those seeking to experience the totality of freedom in the United States of America through the processes of entry appropriated and enforced by law

Unity

- Getting along requires self-denial, introspection, and the actions necessary for us to walk in the Spirit as we strive to impact the culture, but it never includes compromise
- Unity demands forbearance, humility, and the demonstrated love of God Almighty even when we don't feel like it

Epilogue

The last chapter of this book was strategically placed to send you off with a bang! The list of thought-provoking words in chapter 32 and their meanings (my worldview) was a conscientious attempt to get the readers to use their God-given imagination and to think through the issues. I am praying that for those of you who finished the book in its entirety, that you have been energized toward a deeper and more analytical process of thought.

Not all of you will necessarily agree with each jot and tittle of the definitions put forward. By the way, that is precisely the point. Take the time to use critical thinking and analysis to come up with your own definitions. Once you have mastered the skill of dialectic reasoning and thought, take that knowledge and wisdom gleaned from a biblical worldview and apply it in the rhetorical realm.

Take it out for a spin with the confidence that God is preparing you for bigger things. Christian leaders should be comfortable articulating well-reasoned positions on all the issues we face with absolute clarity. In the journey of progressive cultural impact, make a determination to take big leaps of faith. Allow yourself to be stretched for the glory of God. We have little time on this earth and need to get busy making a difference for His Kingdom.

For those of you sitting idly by watching events unfold, I pray this book has inspired you to take action. I believe that Christians have an innate desire toward Kingdom service. Sometimes, all we need is a nudge or tap on the shoulder to send us on our way.

The potential that exists within the imaginations of all Christians is as far as they can see through the wisdom of God's Word.

The discoveries are right there for the asking, receiving, and the doing. Let's get busy! Praise God!

ACKNOWLEDGEMENTS

I want to thank my wife (Calie) for being the first editor and keeping me balanced.

A special thanks to Darren Shearer and his team at High Bridge Books for their attention to detail.

I want to give a shout out to the local coffee shop in the town of Pickens, South Carolina, for allowing me to commandeer a spot for my laptop and set up shop for a while.

Ethan Harbin did another fine job on the graphics for the front cover.

About Us

Christian Leadership Worldview International (clwi.org) offers high-quality leadership training and development solutions at affordable prices. Our desire is to help grow leaders around the world through one conversation at a time. We strive to impact organizations by improving employee morale, reducing turnover, increasing productivity, and fostering collaboration and teamwork as well as creating personal growth and self-improvement opportunities. In addition, CLWI takes a special interest in the development of young student leaders around the world.

Using a non-profit organizational model, CLWI has the flexibility to offer customized leadership solutions through a menu of options while being a low-cost industry provider. We are ready to serve the leadership needs of both employees and students alike. We are a Christian organization that uses Biblical principles and concepts as the foundation for organizational development and key learning experiences. Our focus is to point people to Jesus Christ, and we do it through training and development.

We believe that working through **local churches** is fundamental to who we are as an organization. As we help to grow Christian leaders on the one hand as well as evangelize and spread the gospel message on the other, we want to make sure that everyone is interacting with a local body of Christian believers as the Bible instructs us to do.

Our Logo

The prayer of Christian Leadership Worldview International (clwi.org) and its partners is that the logo represents a bold, compassionate, willing, and activist participant against a backdrop of global organizational need. CLWI wants our logo to signify the desperate need around the world for Christian leadership training and development in small-to-medium-sized organizations. We believe that many organizations of today are being left out of this needed spiritual growth opportunity as they focus primarily on financial, social, environmental, and technological concerns, leaving out the spiritual development of their people.

The silhouette behind the podium in the logo depicts the "call to action" for Christian leaders to stand up and get involved. While leadership does not always mean being front-and-center in a crowd, it does mean teaching, training, challenging, and motivating people to reach new heights of spiritual development. From those who lead through prayers kneeling at a bedside to those who are called to preach and teach the word in front of thousands, we must be willing to move beyond self for the benefit of others.